THE CONVENT COOK

THE
CONVENT
COOK

Divine Meals for Families Large and Small

Maria Tisdall

LOCATION PHOTOGRAPHY BY
Guy Kloppenburg

FOOD PHOTOGRAPHY BY
Ben Fink

TEN SPEED PRESS
Berkeley / Toronto

Ten Speed Press
PO Box 7123
Berkeley, California 94707
www.tenspeed.com

Distributed in Australia by Simon and Schuster Australia, in Canada by Ten Speed Press Canada,
in New Zealand by Southern Publishers Group, in South Africa by Real Books, in Southeast
Asia by Berkeley Books, and in the United Kingdom and Europe by Airlift Book Company.

Cover and text design by Nancy Austin
Food and prop styling by Wesley Martin

Library of Congress Cataloging-in-Publication Data
Tisdall, Maria.
The convent cook : divine meals for families large and small / Maria Tisdall.
p. cm.
Includes index.
ISBN 1-58008-313-7
1. Cookery, American.   2. Cookery, International.   I. Title.
TX715 .T612   2002
641.5973—dc21   2001005552

First printing, 2002
Printed in China

1 2 3 4 5 6 7 8 9 10 — 06 05 04 03 02

A journey would be less memorable without peaks and valleys.

Thank you to my touchstones:
my parents, Helen and Lou;
my husband, Michael;
my most precious gifts, Michael, Matthew, and Hannah;
and most especially,
my personal angel here on earth,
Sister Flavia Mundie, O.S.B.,
without whom none of this would have come to be.

Contents

CONTENTS

Introduction

MY LIFE HAS ALWAYS BEEN BLESSED BY FOOD. Born and raised in Montclair, New Jersey, my formative years were spent learning how to make old-fashioned comfort food under the careful instruction of my mother and grandmother. On a separate front, my father felt it was equally important to experience the ambience and adventure of truly fine dining, so wherever his work took him—Manhattan, Washington, D.C., Los Angeles—we followed and ate. Gradually food became more priority than play, and by the age of sixteen, I was working in a restaurant part time and participating in cooking competitions at New York's Culinary Institute of America (CIA), only to return later to attend its culinary arts program.

Two years after graduating from the CIA, I was through with the restaurant rat race. I had worked in more than ten kitchens, trying to find a restaurant that appreciated my talents and the long hours I put in to make it successful. I had just about given up hope of a career as a chef when I read a small ad in the local paper advertising for a cook at the Saint Walburga Monastery in Elizabeth, New Jersey. The Benedictine Sisters who made the monastery their home had recently lost their main kitchen in a building collapse. Their cook had been unable to adjust to cooking in the backup kitchen, which was housed in a turn-of-the-century mansion. It was clear that the new cook would have many obstacles to overcome.

I knew right away that this was the job for me! I interviewed one day and was making dinner the next for forty Sisters in the dining room plus a twenty-bed infirmary. I was the entire kitchen staff, faced with figuring out refrigeration and storage for all the foodstuffs and with learning the nuances of cooking on a gas range that was older than I was and liked to shoot out fireballs at me as it pleased.

I planned the menus, ordered the food, and received the deliveries. I cooked the meals, served the Sisters, and cleaned up the kitchen. I was in my glory.

The convent has allowed me to keep all of my CIA skills sharp and, unlike my restaurant days, when the only feedback I ever got was when someone was unhappy with a meal and sent it back, here my "customers" appreciate me. Not a day goes by when at least one of the Sisters, if not five or six, doesn't say, "Thank you, thank you, for all that you do. Thank you, the food was delicious." I hadn't realized how much I missed these simple sentiments. Little did the Sisters know it, but with this kind of response, I knew I was here for the duration. In the ensuing twelve years, I have seen a new church built that includes a state-of-the-art professional kitchen, and the Sisters have seen me marry and have welcomed each of my three children warmly into their hearts and home.

Through my service at the convent, I've come to know and appreciate the rich history and tradition of the Benedictine Sisters of Elizabeth, and I want to share as much of it as I can in this book. The first Benedictine Sisters arrived in the United States in 1852, coming from the German city of Eichstatt in Bavaria. They settled in a small town in Pennsylvania, where they started schools and served the community as best they could. Six Sisters were eventually sent to Newark, New Jersey, to establish a convent there. In 1868, three of these Sisters became an independent community and were sent to Elizabeth, where a new convent had been built for them. In this new location, the three Sisters grew to almost one hundred strong. They in turn started several missions, or satellite convents, from which they served the community. One such mission was set up in Ecuador, and with its establishment, the Benedictine Sisters of Elizabeth became the first female Catholic missionaries in that country, where they helped to educate and otherwise serve the people. The Sisters also started and still run the Benedictine hospital in Kingston, New York, which contributes to the medical and spiritual needs of the city.

Since my arrival at the convent, it has been my honor and pleasure to serve these hardworking women through my cooking. I love to cook. I love the rhythm of a recipe from start to finish. I love turning fresh, simple, tasty ingredients into satisfying works of art that everyone can enjoy. When friends and family ask what my secret is, I tell them that I relax and go with the flow. I'm not afraid to cook the way I like to eat, to allow the natural progression of things to contribute to the creation of good food. Too many people get caught up in the details. If you like onions and think a recipe could use more, add more. If you don't like a particular herb or spice, try another in its place. Chances are that you won't ruin anything. Instead, you'll be making the recipe your own.

My second favorite tip to share is the concept of *mise en place,* a practice as useful to home cooks as it is to professionals. This French phrase means total preparation. Get all of your ingredients cleaned, peeled, cored, diced, sliced, and measured before you begin to put the recipe together. Fill a sink with hot soapy water, and the whole cooking and cleaning process becomes neat, simple, and quick.

I believe that the purpose of any good cookbook is to expand knowledge. Whether your level of expertise is simple or gourmet, I hope that this book entices you to explore areas that you may never have tried. For some, that may mean entering the kitchen and using an appliance other than the microwave. For others, it will be discovering a new way to make a simple pot roast or grilled chicken. And for still others, it might involve the use of new and varied ingredients in a never-attempted recipe. I have been in each of these positions. Whether professional or beginner, the main idea is to enjoy yourself and your fellow diners. Share your love of food through these recipes and have a good time.

From the convent's kitchen to your own, I hope these recipes bring as much pleasure and enjoyment to your family and friends as they do to the good Sisters. Bon appétit and God bless!

JANUARY

Around the convent, January is a time of transition. Here we still celebrate the traditional twelve days of Christmas until the Feast of the Epiphany, which falls on January 6 and is regarded as the end of the holiday period. What this means to the Sisters is an extension of the Christmas celebrations and feelings of good cheer for nearly two weeks. The trees stay lit and the richly colored poinsettias remain around the church until January 7. Only then are all of the decorations lovingly taken down and stored away for another year. The Christmas trees and evergreen wreaths that have decked the halls are transformed into mulch, leaving behind their spicy scent as a reminder of the good times experienced over the past several weeks. With all of the excitement over the Christmas celebrations now spent and the New Year successfully ushered in, the Sisters return from their visits to family and friends and are back in school, along with their disenchanted students.

In the kitchen, I take this time to inventory what we have and what we will need over the next few months. I also buy a new calendar with big beautiful pictures for each month and large squares for each day, where I post the menus for each night's dinner. During the day, the Sisters pop into the kitchen to check out the night's menu and enjoy a brightly lit beach scene or a cool mountain range. The calendar also serves as a tool for grocery-list making and for planning what I can do ahead of time, prep wise. Although I generally design the menus on a weekly basis, I also like to think in terms of the four seasons, so that each menu highlights what is seasonally available.

January brings with it cold days and long nights, so I plan meals that incorporate warm and comforting components. Each menu follows a basic formula. We always start with a salad or a light appetizer. Since I am a big fan of salads, occasionally I will plan one hearty enough to serve as a main dish. I use lots of fresh dark greens like spinach or escarole, ingredients rich in nutrients that the Sisters may be lacking at this time of the year. I then add a protein like hard-boiled eggs or aged blue cheese. Finally, I throw in some plum tomatoes and red onion slices, toss everything with a simple vinaigrette, and the result is a salad that eats like a meal.

Next I move on to planning the entrées. I start by deciding what meat I want to use. The Sisters prefer beef, but I try to alternate that at least twice a week with fresh fish or chicken. I will also include a roast pork loin or pork chops with sauerkraut. Leg of lamb or grilled lamb chops have become favorites too, especially when I marinate them with lemon and garlic.

After planning the week's entrées, I move on to the side dishes. Each meal is accompanied by a starch. It may be as simple as a baked potato or as complex as a bubbling pan of homemade macaroni and cheese. Two vegetables are served each night, and one of them is always green. When I was first hired, the Sister who supervised me explained that according to the Rule of Saint Benedict, each dinner meal should always include a choice of two vegetables, one of them green. A choice ensures that every member of the community will be offered something that they like, and they will always remain healthy and well nourished. During January, one vegetable might be green beans, broccoli, or another green. I then plan a dish that takes advantage of the winter crops, like acorn squash or root vegetables such as rutabagas or beets. Many people dismiss these vegetables, considering them hard to prepare or tasteless and boring, but I feel

✝ *Stained glass windows in the church.*

that any fresh ingredient available during the winter should be embraced enthusiastically. While you may not appreciate the delicate sweetness of fresh beets in the middle of the spring and summer produce boom, they are a welcome change from the usual offerings of the freezer section.

Preparing seasonal specialties is just one way to stave off the gloominess of January's long, dark afternoons. It is fulfilling to throw myself into the kitchen and make something warm and tasty for dinner. After all the work is done, the best part is gathering everyone to the table and enjoying one another's company. It makes the days seem longer and the nights shorter.

Spinach and Bacon Salad

SERVES 4 TO 6

This salad truly eats like a meal. Accompany it with a loaf of crusty French bread and you will fulfill anyone's desire for a warm homemade dinner. The Sisters particularly like to come home from school and smell the aroma of bacon drifting down the hall.

DRESSING

2 teaspoons grated yellow onion
1 teaspoon salt
1/2 teaspoon freshly ground black pepper
2 tablespoons Dijon mustard
2 tablespoons tarragon vinegar
1/2 cup extra virgin olive oil
1/2 teaspoon freshly squeezed lemon juice

10 ounces spinach
6 slices bacon, cut crosswise into 1/2-inch strips
6 to 8 button mushrooms, sliced
1/2 red onion, thinly sliced
3 hard-boiled eggs, peeled and chopped

To prepare the dressing, in a food processor or blender, combine the yellow onion, salt, pepper, mustard, and vinegar. Process for 1 to 2 minutes, until smooth. With the motor running, slowly add the oil to create an emulsion. Pour the dressing into a small bowl and stir in the lemon juice. Taste and adjust the seasoning if necessary. Cover with plastic wrap and set aside.

To prepare the salad, immerse the spinach in a large amount of water, swish the leaves to rinse well, and drain. Repeat until no grit or dirt is visible in the bottom of the sink or basin. Pick off any large or thick stems and tear the leaves into bite-sized pieces. Dry in a lettuce spinner and transfer to a large salad bowl. Cover with a damp paper towel and place in the refrigerator until ready to serve.

About 20 minutes before serving, in a small sauté pan over medium heat, sauté the bacon for 5 to 6 minutes, until crisp. Remove the spinach from the refrigerator, add the mushrooms, red onion, and eggs to the bowl, and toss. Add the dressing and toss again. Remove the bacon from the pan with a large slotted spoon, draining well, and add to the salad. Toss well.

Serve immediately, preferably while the bacon is still sizzling. Or add the bacon tableside and watch your guests' reactions to the crackle of hot bacon on the chilled greens.

Balsamic Chicken with Pears

SERVES 4 TO 6

In this recipe, the balsamic vinegar not only tenderizes the chicken to a buttery consistency, but also lends a sweet-and-sour taste to the sauce. As my children can attest, the cherries add a splash of color and sweetness that makes this dish appealing to even the pickiest eaters.

6 boneless, skinless chicken breast halves
Salt
Freshly ground black pepper
2 tablespoons vegetable oil
1 shallot, chopped
2 pears, peeled, cored, and sliced
1 cup chicken stock (page 197)
1/4 cup balsamic vinegar
2 tablespoons sugar
2 teaspoons cornstarch
1/2 cup dried cherries

Rinse the chicken under cold running water and pat dry with paper towels. One at a time, place the chicken breasts between 2 sheets of plastic wrap. Using a meat mallet, carefully pound the breasts to a uniform thickness of about 1/2 inch. Season on both sides with salt and pepper.

Heat a large sauté pan over high heat and add the oil. When the oil is hot, add the chicken and sauté, turning once, for 3 to 4 minutes on each side, until golden brown. Transfer to a plate and cover to keep warm. To the same pan, add the shallot and sauté over high heat for 2 minutes, until soft. Decrease the heat to medium and add the pears. Continue sautéing, stirring occasionally, for 3 to 4 minutes, until the pears are soft and golden brown.

To prepare the sauce, combine the stock, vinegar, sugar, and cornstarch in a small bowl. Pour over the pear mixture and add the cherries. Increase the heat to high and simmer, stirring frequently, for 6 to 8 minutes, until the sauce thickens slightly. Return the chicken and any juices to the pan. Bring the mixture back to a simmer and decrease the heat to medium. Cook for 10 minutes, until the chicken is cooked through and no longer pink, then taste and adjust the seasoning if necessary.

Place the chicken on a warmed large platter. With a slotted spoon, mound the fruit over the top. Spoon the sauce over the fruit and around the breasts. Serve immediately.

Your way of acting should be different from the world's way;
the love of Christ must come before all else. You are not to act
in anger or nurse a grudge.

—The Rule of Saint Benedict, chapter 4

Roast Pork Loin with Olives and Capers *(see photo insert)*

SERVES 4 TO 6

When I came up with this recipe, the Sisters thought I had gone off the culinary deep end. "Brown sugar and garlic?" they exclaimed. "It will never work!" But boy oh boy does it! Legend has it that there were tongue marks on the plates at meal's end the first time I served this dish. The added zing of the capers and olives will brighten up any winter's night.

1 (2- to 3-pound) boneless pork loin
1/2 cup firmly packed brown sugar
3 cloves garlic, finely chopped
2 teaspoons salt
1 teaspoon freshly ground black pepper
1/4 cup olive oil
1 cup dry white wine
1 cup chicken stock (page 197)
2 tablespoons cornstarch
1 teaspoon dried oregano
1/2 cup raisins
1/4 cup chopped green olives
2 tablespoons capers

Preheat the oven to 350°. To prepare the roast, rinse the loin under cold running water and pat dry with paper towels. In a small bowl, mix together the brown sugar, garlic, salt, pepper, and oil. Rub the mixture all over the roast, spreading it as evenly as possible. Place in a heavy roasting pan.

Place in the oven and roast for 60 to 90 minutes, until the roast reaches an internal temperature of 160°. Remove from the oven and transfer to a warmed large platter. Loosely tent with aluminum foil to keep warm.

To prepare the sauce, drain the liquid from the roasting pan and place the pan on the stovetop over medium heat. Add the wine and deglaze the pan, scraping up any brown bits with a wooden spatula. Simmer over medium heat, stirring occasionally, for 10 minutes, until reduced by half. In a small bowl, combine the stock, cornstarch, and oregano. Add to the pan along with the raisins, olives, and capers. Bring to a boil, then decrease the heat to medium-low and simmer gently, stirring occasionally, for 10 minutes, until thickened. Taste and adjust the seasoning if necessary.

To serve, slice the roast into $1/2$-inch-thick pieces, being careful not to tear the crust. Stir any accumulated meat juices from the platter into the sauce. Place 2 slices of meat on each dinner plate. Drizzle the sauce over the meat and serve immediately.

Roast Beef with an Herbed Rub

SERVES 4 TO 6

Almost every Sunday, the Sisters celebrate with a roast beef dinner. Traditionally the Sunday meal is served early, so that the Sisters are left with an open afternoon. They use this free time for personal tasks, visiting friends, or private reflection.

1 (2- to 3-pound) beef top round roast
1/2 cup vegetable oil
2 teaspoons salt
1 teaspoon freshly ground black pepper
1 teaspoon garlic powder
1 teaspoon paprika
1 tablespoon fresh thyme leaves, or 1 teaspoon dried thyme
1 tablespoon fresh rosemary leaves, or 1 teaspoon dried rosemary
2 to 3 tablespoons flour
1/2 cup dry red wine
2 cups beef stock (page 199)

Preheat the oven to 350°. To prepare the roast, rinse the beef under cold running water and pat dry with paper towels. In a small bowl, mix together the oil, salt, pepper, garlic powder, paprika, thyme, and rosemary. Rub the mixture all over the beef, spreading it as evenly as possible. Place in a roasting pan.

Place in the oven and roast for 60 to 90 minutes, until the roast reaches an internal temperature of 165° for medium well, or until desired doneness. Remove from the oven and transfer to a warmed large platter. Loosely tent with aluminum foil to keep warm.

To prepare the gravy, place the roasting pan on the stovetop over medium heat. Whisk 2 tablespoons of the flour into the pan juices to form a smooth paste.

Add the remaining 1 tablespoon flour if the mixture seems too wet. Add the wine and stock, increase the heat to high, and bring to a boil. Decrease the heat to medium-low and whisk constantly for about 10 minutes, until thickened to the consistency of light cream. Remove from the heat and pass through a fine-mesh sieve. Taste and adjust the seasoning if necessary. Pour into a warmed gravy boat or bowl.

To serve, slice the roast thinly. Stir any accumulated meat juices from the platter into the gravy. Serve the meat on the platter with the gravy on the side.

The workshop where we are to toil faithfully at all of these tasks
is the enclosure of the monastery and stability in the community.

—**The Rule of Saint Benedict, chapter 4**

Whipped Potatoes

SERVES 4 TO 6

The Sisters *love* their whipped potatoes, so what better accompaniment to a big Sunday dinner? Combining two types of potatoes brings the best features of each to the dish. Boiling potatoes have a higher sugar content, which improves the taste, while baking potatoes have a higher starch content, which improves the texture. To spice them up, sometimes I add roasted garlic or Cheddar cheese and sour cream. But plain or fancy, they are the perfect complement to any savory sauce.

1 pound boiling potatoes, unpeeled
1 pound baking potatoes, unpeeled
Salt
1/4 cup unsalted butter
1 cup milk
Freshly ground black pepper
Chopped fresh parsley, for garnish

Place the potatoes in a large pot, add cold water to cover, and bring to a rolling boil over high heat. Add several pinches of salt and decrease the heat to medium. Simmer, uncovered, for 30 minutes, until fork tender.

Meanwhile, in a small saucepan over low heat, combine the butter and milk and heat until the butter is melted and the milk warmed through. When the potatoes are ready, drain and place in a large bowl. With an electric mixer on low speed, break up the potatoes until they begin to mash. Add the milk-butter mixture and continue to mix on low speed until well incorporated. Season with salt and pepper and whip on high speed until light and fluffy.

Transfer the potatoes to a warmed large serving bowl and garnish with the parsley. Serve immediately.

Pearl Onions with Orange Glaze

SERVES 4 TO 6

Glazed vegetables are the epitome of comfort food. Their soft texture and sweet taste enhance simpler entrées. I use sweet pearl onions as a departure from the typical root vegetables, but parboiled carrots or beets could easily be substituted.

2 pounds pearl onions, skin on
2 tablespoons unsalted butter
2 teaspoons olive oil
2 tablespoons sugar
1/2 teaspoon ground nutmeg
1/2 cup freshly squeezed orange juice
1/4 cup balsamic vinegar
Salt
Freshly ground white pepper

Bring a saucepan full of water to a boil over high heat. Add the onions and blanch for 1 to 2 minutes, until slightly tender. Drain the onions, then cut off the root and stem ends. To free the onions from their skins, pinch each on one end—the peeled onion should pop out.

In a large sauté pan over high heat, melt the butter with the oil. Add the onions and sauté for 4 to 5 minutes, until golden brown. Decrease the heat to medium and sprinkle with the sugar and nutmeg. Sauté for 1 minute, until the nutmeg releases its aroma. Add the orange juice and vinegar and sauté for 7 to 8 minutes, until the sauce reduces to a glaze and the onions are tender.

Season with salt and pepper and serve in a warmed serving bowl.

The Creamiest Dreamiest Cheesecake Ever

SERVES 8 TO 10

My mother has perfected this recipe over the years by making it for our family's annual New Year's celebration. The Sisters have since adopted it as their own. It is the only cheesecake I have ever tasted that is neither too sweet nor too heavy. The absence of flour in the filling lends a particularly creamy texture. For an added flourish, serve with sweetened whipped cream, sliced strawberries, or crushed pineapple.

CRUST

1 1/2 cups graham cracker crumbs
1/4 cup sugar
1/4 cup unsalted butter, at room temperature

FILLING

4 (8-ounce) packages cream cheese, at room temperature
6 eggs
2 teaspoons pure vanilla extract
2 cups sugar
2 pints (4 cups) sour cream

Preheat the oven to 350°. Grease a 9-inch springform pan with butter.

To prepare the crust, in a bowl, combine the crumbs, sugar, and butter and mix until the mixture has the consistency of rolled oats. Transfer to the prepared pan and press onto the bottom and all the way up the sides to form a crust. Carefully line with aluminum foil and fill with pie weights or dried beans. Bake for 12 minutes, until golden brown. Remove from the oven and place on a cooling rack for 10 minutes. Carefully remove the pie weights and foil and allow to cool completely on the cooling rack.

To prepare the filling, place the cream cheese in a large bowl. With an electric mixer on high speed, beat until light, fluffy, and smooth. Scrape down the sides of the bowl. With the mixer on low speed, add the eggs one at a time, scraping down the sides of the bowl after each addition. Mix in the vanilla and scrape down the sides of the bowl. With the mixer still on low speed, slowly add the sugar and beat until light and creamy. Scrape down the sides of the bowl. In a separate bowl, whisk the sour cream until it is completely smooth. Add the sour cream to the cream cheese mixture and beat on medium speed until completely incorporated. Scrape down the sides of the bowl once more and pour the filling into the crust.

Bake for 1 to 1 1/4 hours at 350°, until the center is set but not firm (the center should jiggle slightly when the cake is shaken). Turn off the heat, open the oven door slightly, and leave the cake in the oven for 1 hour. Transfer to a cooling rack and let cool completely. Refrigerate overnight, then cut into thin slices to serve.

The convent is located on a tree-lined street in a city that has been growing and evolving ever since George Washington took up residency there during the Revolutionary War.

The architecture of the facilities reflects the years that have gone by as the Benedictine Sisters have been busy making their mark on the area. The original building, a gorgeous stone mansion designed by noted American architect Stanford White, housed the Sisters from 1923 until 1968 (the convent was founded in 1868, but only moved to the current site with the completion of this building). The mansion is complemented by a sunken garden and was originally surrounded by eleven acres of land. Its twenty-five rooms offer, among other things, parquet floors and a mahogany-paneled dining room that reflects the grandeur of the period.

In 1968, a new motherhouse complex was dedicated. This facility offered residence buildings, an infirmary, a new kitchen and dining room, and a 250-seat church. Unfortunately some of these buildings did not stand the test of time and in March 1990, the church collapsed under the stress of poor building materials. From the ashes of this tragedy, a new era of the convent has been born. In 1993, a rebuilt church was dedicated; its foundations adjoin those of the buildings from the previous two facilities. The new church is bright, airy, and resplendent with the light that filters through the beautiful stained glass windows. The old gardens of the mansion were combined with new plantings outside the church to form a beautiful rose garden with a gurgling fountain and benches for quiet reflection. A new kitchen was designed with my help, supplemented by a newly reconfigured dining room that can seat up to one hundred of the Sisters and their family and friends for special events. The base of the collapsed church has been redesigned to house a community center, upholstery

✠ *The mansion.*

shop, and preschool. Each of these endeavors has successfully served the Sisters and the surrounding community for the past eight years and will continue to do so for many more to come.

FEBRUARY

Although winter's chill still lingers in the air, all thoughts turn to love in the month of February. While the Sisters are busy remembering their loved ones with cards and small gifts, I try to remember each of the Sisters with little acts of culinary kindness. I serve them their favorites, whether for dinner or dessert. It is my way of showing them how special they are to me.

I have always shown my affection through food. As a little girl, I stirred up simple meals and baked my family's favorite cookies and brownies. Showing someone you care is easy with a freshly baked chocolate chip cookie. I brought this trait with me to the convent's kitchen. Over the years, I have come to know each of the Sister's likes and dislikes. During this month, I try to concentrate on their top choices. I offer favorite menu items, of course, but I also make sure to have on hand the product brands the Sisters prefer. When ordering produce, fresh and frozen dairy products, dry goods, and other supplies I try to remember to include Sister Janice's frozen fudge bars or the right brand of peanut butter for Sister Flavia. When planning meals, I prepare the pot roast just the way Sister Pierre likes it, and then slice it by hand the way her sister, Sister Francine, prefers.

When drawing up February's calendar, I tend toward dishes built on multi-layered flavors. Lots of snow and freezing temperatures make February menus more difficult, but I don't let that or the lack of abundant fresh produce stop me from preparing generous salads and side dishes. The Sisters love my recipe for Goldfish Salad. An added bonus is that its mandarin oranges and red onions can be found at any time of the year. These ingredients, paired with crisp romaine lettuce and a hearty balsamic vinaigrette, make the salad a taste treat. When preparing my pot roast, I braise it first and then use the braising liquid to cook the vegetables and make the gravy. My pork chops with caramelized onions and sauerkraut are a favorite with many of the Sisters. This recipe uses the sweet flavor of the onions to complement the tart, salty sauerkraut. Serve this dish with baby lima beans and wild rice, and your family will forever sing your culinary praise.

For dessert, my Cut-It-Out Sugar Cookies always top the list. Their crisp, buttery texture with a hint of lemon are especially good with a hot cup of tea and the company of someone special. Culinary kindnesses are always the best way to say I love you.

Give us this day our daily bread.

—The Lord's Prayer

Goldfish Salad

SERVES 4 TO 6

When I developed the recipe for this salad, I asked one of the Sisters what she would call it. She replied that the oranges reminded her of goldfish swimming in a pond, hence the name.

1 head Romaine lettuce
1/2 cup sliced almonds

DRESSING
2 tablespoons balsamic vinegar
2 tablespoons white wine vinegar
2 tablespoons sugar
2 teaspoons Dijon mustard
1 shallot, minced
2/3 cup extra virgin olive oil
Salt
Freshly ground black pepper

1 red onion, thinly sliced
1 (4-ounce) can mandarin oranges, chilled and drained

Preheat the oven to 350°.

Chop the lettuce into bite-sized pieces, rinse thoroughly in a large amount of water, and drain. Dry in a lettuce spinner and transfer to a large salad bowl. Cover with a damp paper towel and place in the refrigerator until ready to serve.

To toast the almonds, spread them on a small baking sheet in a single layer. Place in the oven and toast for 8 to 10 minutes, until golden brown. Remove from the oven and pour onto a plate to cool.

(continued)

To prepare the dressing, in a small bowl, whisk together the vinegars, sugar, mustard, and shallot. While whisking briskly, slowly add the olive oil to form an emulsion. Season with salt and pepper to taste.

Remove the lettuce from the refrigerator and add the onion, oranges, and almonds, reserving some of the almonds for garnish. Add the dressing and toss well. Garnish with the reserved almonds and serve.

Two kinds of cooked food, therefore, should suffice for all, and if fruit or fresh vegetables are available, a third dish may be added.

—The Rule of Saint Benedict, chapter 39

Chicken Aegean

SERVES 4 TO 6

The combination of garlic, oregano, and lemon forms a crispy crust on the chicken pieces and creates a sauce that is delicious served over rice. It goes especially well with Almond-Scented Rice Pilaf (page 31).

4 bone-in chicken breasts halves, skin on
4 chicken thighs, skin on
4 drumsticks, skin on
3/4 to 1 cup freshly squeezed lemon juice
1 teaspoon salt
1 teaspoon freshly ground black pepper
1 teaspoon garlic powder
1 teaspoon dried oregano
1 teaspoon paprika

Preheat the oven to 350°. Rinse the chicken pieces under cold running water and pat dry with paper towels. Place the chicken pieces, skin side up, in a roasting pan. Pour the lemon juice over, using enough to cover each piece. Sprinkle the chicken evenly with the salt, pepper, garlic powder, oregano, and paprika. Place in the oven and roast for 35 to 45 minutes, until golden brown and crispy.

Transfer the chicken to a warmed platter and tent loosely with aluminum foil to keep warm. Pour the pan juices into a warmed bowl and skim off as much fat as possible. Taste and adjust the seasoning with salt and pepper if necessary. Serve immediately with the sauce on the side.

Braised Pot Roast with Roasted Vegetables

SERVES 4 TO 6

I often serve this pot roast when the weather is cold and the Sisters are in need of a dose of comfort. The slow-cooking of the meat and vegetables yields an entrée that is both tasty and good for the soul.

1 large yellow onion, thickly sliced
1 (2- to 3-pound) beef top round or rump roast
1 cup flour
1 tablespoon salt
1 teaspoon freshly ground black pepper
1 tablespoon garlic powder
1 teaspoon paprika
1 teaspoon dried thyme
1/4 cup vegetable oil
4 small white onions
6 Red Bliss potatoes, peeled
4 carrots, peeled and cut crosswise into thirds
4 celery stalks, quartered crosswise
About 4 cups beef stock (page 199)
1 cup water

Preheat the oven to 350°. Layer the onion slices in the bottom of a large roasting pan. Rinse the roast under cold water and pat dry with paper towels. On a large piece of waxed paper, mix together 1/2 cup of the flour, the salt, pepper, garlic powder, paprika, and thyme. Dredge the roast in the flour mixture and allow to set for 10 minutes.

Heat a large sauté pan over high heat and add the oil. When the oil is hot, dredge the roast one more time and shake off the excess flour. Place the roast in the pan and sear on all sides for about 5 minutes, until golden brown. Transfer to the prepared roasting pan. Sprinkle the small onions, potatoes, carrots, and celery around the roast. Season the vegetables with salt and pepper.

In a saucepan over high heat, bring the stock to a gentle boil. Pour enough stock into the roasting pan to reach halfway up the sides of the roast. Cover the pan tightly with aluminum foil. Place in the oven and braise for $1^{1}/_{2}$ to 2 hours, until the meat is fork tender. Remove from the oven and allow to rest for 30 minutes before uncovering and removing from the pan.

Transfer the roast to a warmed platter and tent loosely with aluminum foil to keep warm. With a slotted spoon, transfer the vegetables to a serving dish, cover, and keep warm. Place the roasting pan and its juices on the stovetop over high heat and bring to a boil. In a small bowl, combine the remaining $1/2$ cup flour and the water and whisk until there are no lumps. Decrease the heat to medium and add the flour-water mixture. Stir constantly with a wooden or heatproof plastic spatula (a metal spatula will impart a metallic taste to the gravy) for 2 to 3 minutes, until thickened to a good consistency. Pour the gravy through a fine-mesh sieve into a warmed gravy boat or bowl. Taste and adjust the seasoning with salt and pepper if necessary.

To serve, cut the roast into $1/2$-inch-thick slices and place on the platter. Surround the meat with the warm vegetables and drizzle with a little of the gravy. Serve immediately, accompanied with the remaining gravy.

Pork Chops with Sauerkraut and Caramelized Onions

SERVES 6

At least once a month, one of the Sisters asks if this dish will be on the menu. Often I will bump another entrée to squeeze in this heartwarming favorite.

6 center-cut pork chops
1/2 cup flour
1 teaspoon salt
1 teaspoon freshly ground black pepper
1 teaspoon garlic powder
1 teaspoon paprika
Vegetable oil, for sautéing
1 tablespoon unsalted butter
2 large yellow onions, sliced
1 teaspoon caraway seeds
1 (16-ounce) container deli sauerkraut

Rinse the pork chops under cold running water and pat dry with paper towels. In a large, resealable plastic bag, combine the flour, salt, pepper, garlic powder, and paprika. One at a time, place the chops in the bag and shake to coat. Heat a large sauté pan over high heat and add enough oil to coat the bottom. When the oil is hot, add the chops and sauté, turning once, for 4 to 5 minutes per side, until golden brown and cooked through. Transfer to a warmed plate and keep warm.

Drain the oil from the pan. Add the butter to the same pan over medium heat. Add the onions and caraway seeds and sauté for 15 to 20 minutes, until the onions are browned and caramelized. Add the sauerkraut and stir well. Return the pork chops to the pan, cover, and simmer over medium heat for 20 minutes, until most of the moisture is reduced and a sauce has formed. To serve, spoon the sauerkraut and onions onto a warmed platter or large dish. Arrange the chops on top and serve piping hot.

Almond-Scented Rice Pilaf

SERVES 4 TO 6

Basmati rice adds a subtle nutty flavor to this pilaf. It can therefore stand up to a full-flavored dish like Pork Chops with Sauerkraut and Caramelized Onions (opposite page) or enhance a simpler dish like Chicken Aegean (page 27).

2 tablespoons unsalted butter
1/4 cup finely diced yellow onion
1/2 cup slivered blanched almonds
2 cups basmati rice
4 cups chicken stock (page 197)
1/4 teaspoon salt

In a saucepan over medium heat, slowly melt the butter without browning. Add the onion and almonds, stir to coat, and sauté for 8 minutes, until the almonds are golden brown. Add the rice and stir to coat each grain with butter. Add the stock and salt and increase the heat to high. Cover and bring to a boil. Decrease the heat to low and simmer slowly for 20 minutes, until all the moisture has been absorbed and the grains are tender.

Remove the rice from the heat and fluff with a fork before serving.

Oven-Roasted Marinated Vegetables

SERVES 4 TO 6

When looking for fresh produce in February, one can usually find zucchini and yellow squashes. This recipe reminds us that the days of summer—when we can move the vegetables to the grill—are not too far off.

1 (8-ounce) jar oil-packed sundried tomatoes
1 teaspoon salt
1/2 teaspoon freshly ground black pepper
1 tablespoon fresh oregano, or 1 teaspoon dried oregano
1/2 teaspoon paprika
3 cloves garlic, chopped
1 pound zucchini, chopped
1 pound yellow squashes, chopped
2 large yellow onions, chopped
1 green bell pepper, stemmed, seeded, and chopped
1 red bell pepper, stemmed, seeded, and chopped

Drain the oil from the sundried tomatoes into a small bowl. Chop the tomatoes into small pieces. Add the salt, pepper, oregano, paprika, and garlic to the reserved tomato oil.

In a large bowl, toss together the sundried tomatoes, zucchini, yellow squashes, onions, and green and red bell peppers. Add the oil mixture and toss well. Cover with plastic wrap and marinate in the refrigerator for 20 minutes.

Preheat the oven to 350°. Line a baking sheet with aluminum foil and grease with oil. Spread the vegetables in an even layer on the prepared baking sheet. Roast for 30 to 45 minutes, turning every 15 minutes, until browned and fork tender. Transfer the vegetables to a warmed shallow bowl and serve.

Cut-It-Out Sugar Cookies *(see photo insert)*

MAKES 2 DOZEN SMALL COOKIES

When these cookies are cut into hearts of all sizes and decorated with colored sugars or ornamental icing, they make wonderful St. Valentine's Day presents. Whether for your special someone, or for a group of sixty nuns, these sugary cutouts are a gift that comes straight from the heart.

1 cup unsalted butter, at room temperature
1 cup granulated sugar
1 egg
1 teaspoon pure lemon extract
1 tablespoon grated lemon zest
2$3/4$ cups flour
2 teaspoons baking powder
Pinch of salt
Colored sugars and sprinkles, for decorating (optional)

ICING (OPTIONAL)
1$1/4$ cups confectioners' sugar, sifted
1 egg white
$1/8$ teaspoon cream of tartar
Food coloring (optional)

Preheat the oven to 400°. Have ready an ungreased baking sheet.

To prepare the cookies, in a large bowl, cream together the butter and granulated sugar with a wooden spoon, until smooth. Stir in the egg. Add the lemon extract and zest and mix well. Set aside.

(continued)

In a sifter, combine the flour, baking powder, and salt. Sift into the wet ingredients and mix together with the spoon until a smooth dough forms. Turn out onto a floured work surface and roll out into a rectangle 1/4 inch thick. Using different-sized small heart-shaped cutters, cut out cookies. Place them on the baking sheet. If you will not be icing the cookies, decorate them with colored sugars or sprinkles. If you will be icing the cookies, bake them plain.

Place in the oven and bake for 8 to 10 minutes, until the edges are golden brown. Remove from the oven and transfer to cooling racks to cool.

To prepare the icing, combine the confectioners' sugar, egg white, cream of tartar, and food coloring in a bowl. Beat with an electric mixer on high speed until light and fluffy. Immediately spread on the cooled cookies, as the icing will harden quickly if exposed to air. If you are interrupted, as I guarantee you will be, cover the icing bowl with a damp cloth.

Store the cookies in an airtight container at room temperature for up to 1 week.

✠ *The statue of Saint Joseph and the child Jesus stands quietly in the rose garden.*

The prioress is the administrative and spiritual head of the convent community. In days gone by, she was called the Reverend Mother and assumed an almost parental role over the Sisters in her charge. Over the years, prioresses have been expected to be strong leaders in both good and bad times.

Mother Walburga Hock was the first prioress; she served the community from 1868 until 1913. During these early years, the community had many obstacles to overcome. At times, the Sisters had little food and no money to buy any. Mother Walburga used the talents and abilities of the young community to find ways to produce handmade items that could be sold in the surrounding community to raise capital to pay for basic necessities. A hundred years later, another prioress, Sister Germaine Fritz, was faced with an equally great challenge. In March 1990, the building housing the church and dining facilities collapsed due to faulty construction. Sister Germaine had to immediately calm

✝ *The back of the mansion viewed from the gardens.*

the fears of the community, and then gather all of her strength and resources to rebuild.

Currently, Sister Louise Garley holds the office of prioress and does so with great strength and grace. Sister Louise is faced with changing times as the community ages and new entrants are few. She guides the Sisters while maintaining a deep respect for the past and a clear plan for the future. Then, in her spare five minutes, she takes the time each day to visit with my son Matthew for special snacks and a quick game of hide-and-seek.

With the passage of years, the Sisters' roles have evolved in the community, and now the job of the prioress is to lead the Sisters into each new day. As the outside world constantly changes, so does the role of the Sisters in it. I think a successful prioress is one who leads the community in a direction that most benefits the surrounding neighborhoods. Such actions reward the Sisters with the satisfaction of having successfully served those around them and, in doing so, having served God.

MARCH

March is traditionally known as the month that comes in like a lion and leaves like a lamb. More years than not, the convent experiences a large snowfall some time during the early part of the month. Then the wind blows hard, the sun gets warmer, and by the time the thirty-first rolls around, spring has sprung and we are cutting pussy willow and looking forward to the forsythias blooming.

The Sisters plan many retreats at the convent each year, and participation in March retreats is particularly popular. Visitors come to the convent and stay for the weekend. They attend lectures on specific topics, share meals, and follow the Sisters' daily prayer schedule. It is a wonderful way to spend quality personal time while absorbing some of the peace and tranquility that the convent has to offer.

As the seventeenth of March nears, a feeling of excitement enters the halls. Many of the Sisters were either born in Ireland or are first-generation daughters, so the Saint Patrick's Day celebrations hold a special place in their hearts. In this area of New Jersey, each town holds a parade and people flock to the many Irish events, where bag pipers and step dancers appear at every turn. The menus are lively, with traditional corned beef and cabbage or roasted leg of lamb always top choices.

We are now deep into the Lenten season, and the convent's menus are more subdued. Light evening meals, plain desserts, and, of course no meat on Fridays are all signs of the sacrifices we make during the forty days preceding Easter. Although the way that I plan my menus has to conform to these limits, there is also something renewing about simplifying your life during this time of year. While the meals take on an almost childlike simplicity, they allow the true tastes and textures of the ingredients to shine. Now is the time to appreciate many of the foods that may have been forgotten over the past year. Buttered toast with cinnamon sugar and a cup of tea, vanilla yogurt with fresh fruit and crunchy granola, and a flounder fillet broiled with lemon are some of the more straightforward menu items that the Sisters enjoy during the Lenten season.

We take this time to reflect on the bounty that God has provided us. How we choose to manipulate these components, how we mix and match them, how we prepare and consume them are all up to us. The simpler the ingredients, the easier it is to create beautiful, nutritious, tasty meals.

While we guard ourselves at every moment from sins and vices

of thought and tongue, of hand or foot, of self will or desires,

let us recall that we are always seen by God in the heavens,

that our actions everywhere are in God's sight and are reported

by the angels at every hour.

—**The Rule of Saint Benedict, chapter 7**

Caesar Salad

SERVES 6 TO 8

What better time of the year to serve this delicious salad than on the Ides of March? This recipe also comes in handy as a perfect first course before Sister Patrick's Spaghetti (page 43).

2 heads romaine lettuce
1 egg
1 clove garlic
Juice of 1 lemon
1/2 cup grated Romano cheese
5 anchovy fillets
2 teaspoons Worcestershire sauce
1/4 teaspoon freshly ground black pepper
1/2 teaspoon dry mustard
1/2 cup extra virgin olive oil
Salt
4 stale slices Italian-style bread
1/4 cup olive oil
1 teaspoon garlic salt

Chop the lettuce into bite-sized pieces, rinse thoroughly in a large amount of water, and drain. Dry in a lettuce spinner and transfer to a large salad bowl. Cover with a damp paper towel and place in the refrigerator until ready to serve.

To prepare the dressing, place the egg in a small saucepan and add cold water to cover. Place the pan over high heat and bring to a rolling boil. Remove the egg immediately. (The egg is now coddled and safe to consume.) Crack the egg into a food processor or blender and add the garlic, lemon juice, cheese, anchovies, Worcestershire sauce, pepper, and mustard. Process on high speed, stopping once to scrape down the sides of the bowl. With the motor on low speed, slowly add the 1/2 cup extra virgin olive oil and blend until thoroughly incorporated and emulsified. Taste and adjust the seasoning with salt and pepper if necessary.

To prepare the croutons, preheat the broiler. Lay the bread slices on an ungreased baking sheet. In a small bowl, combine the 1/4 cup olive oil and the garlic salt. Brush both sides of the bread slices with the oil mixture. Place under the broiler and toast until golden brown. Watch very carefully, as the slices will toast quickly. When the first side is toasted, turn the slices over and toast the other side. Remove from the oven and allow to cool. Cut off the crusts and cut the remaining bread into 1/2-inch squares.

To serve, remove the lettuce from the refrigerator and add the croutons. Drizzle the dressing over and toss well. Serve immediately.

Sister Patrick's Spaghetti with Mixed Italian Meats

SERVES 6 TO 8

Every year, Sister Patrick's feast day falls, of course, on Saint Patrick's Day. In the tradition of other strong Irish women who have gone before her, it is her prerogative to choose the menu for dinner, and that she does, selecting this tasty Italian dish over the traditional corned beef and cabbage.

MEATBALLS
1 pound ground beef
1 cup milk
2 cups seasoned bread crumbs
1/2 cup grated Romano cheese
1 teaspoon salt
1 teaspoon freshly ground black pepper
1 teaspoon fresh oregano leaves, or 1/2 teaspoon dried oregano
1 teaspoon chopped fresh basil, or 1/2 teaspoon dried basil
2 teaspoons chopped fresh parsley
1 teaspoon garlic powder

SAUCE
1 pound mild Italian sausage
1/4 cup olive oil
2 cloves garlic, finely minced
1 large yellow onion, finely chopped
2 (2-ounce) cans tomato paste
2 (28-ounce) cans high-quality Italian diced tomatoes
2 (28-ounce) cans high-quality Italian crushed tomatoes
2 cups water
2 teaspoons salt
1 teaspoon freshly ground black pepper
1/4 cup chopped fresh parsley

(continued)

2 tablespoons fresh oregano leaves, or 1 tablespoon dried oregano
1 tablespoon minced fresh rosemary, or 1 teaspoon dried rosemary
1/4 cup sliced fresh basil, or 1 tablespoon dried basil

2 pounds dried spaghetti
Grated Romano cheese, for garnish

Preheat the oven to 350°. Line a baking sheet with aluminum foil and grease with olive oil.

To prepare the meatballs, in a large bowl, combine the ground beef, milk, bread crumbs, cheese, salt, pepper, oregano, basil, parsley, and garlic powder. Mix together until well blended. Form into 12 meatballs, each about 2 inches in diameter. Place on the prepared baking sheet. Bake for about 20 minutes, until golden brown on the outside. Remove from the oven and allow to cool.

To prepare the sauce, cut each sausage into 3-inch lengths. Prick each piece with a fork to allow steam to escape, also allowing for less shrinkage. Heat a large saucepan over high heat and add the oil. When the oil is hot, add the sausage. Decrease the heat to medium, and cook, turning as needed, for 8 to 10 minutes, until browned on all sides. Transfer to a plate.

Add the garlic and onion to the same pan over medium heat and sauté for 3 to 4 minutes, until aromatic. Cover, decrease the heat to low, and let them sweat for 5 minutes, until soft. Add the tomato paste and cook for 2 to 3 minutes, stirring constantly. Add the diced tomatoes, crushed tomatoes, water, salt, pepper, parsley, oregano, and rosemary. Increase the heat to high and bring to a simmer. Add the meatballs and the sausage to the sauce and bring back to a simmer. Decrease the heat to low and allow to cook slowly, uncovered, for 45 to 60 minutes. Add the basil and simmer for an additional 15 minutes. Taste and adjust the seasoning if necessary.

About 15 minutes before the sauce is ready, bring a large pot of salted water to a boil over high heat. Add the pasta and cook according to the package instructions, until al dente.

Ladle several spoonfuls of the sauce into a warmed large bowl. Drain the pasta and place in the bowl with the sauce. Toss well and transfer to a large serving platter. Surround the pasta with the meatballs, sausage, and remaining sauce, and garnish with the cheese.

Flounder Stuffed with the Devil

SERVES 6

Serving fish on Fridays is a tradition that has endured over time. Although not considered necessary most of the year, the custom is strictly adhered to during Lent. This recipe is an ode to the time I spent working in South Carolina. There I learned first hand about delicious deviled crabs and shrimp. Now I use the same technique to spice up what could otherwise be a bland Friday-night menu. When preparing this recipe for the Sisters, I typically use crabmeat substitute because of budgetary concerns. In a perfect world, fresh crab would always be used. This dish is typically served with boiled potatoes, corn on the cob, and coleslaw.

1 pound cooked crabmeat
1/2 cup chopped green bell pepper
1/2 cup chopped yellow onion
1/2 cup mayonnaise
1/4 cup yellow mustard
1 cup seasoned bread crumbs, or as needed
Salt
Freshly ground black pepper
6 (4- to 5-ounce) flounder fillets
Paprika, for sprinkling

Preheat the oven to 350°. Grease a 9 by 13-inch glass or ceramic baking dish.

To prepare the stuffing, place the crabmeat in a food processor. Pulse about 5 times, until finely chopped. Transfer to a large bowl. Place the bell pepper and onion in the food processor. Pulse about 5 times, until finely chopped. Remove from the processor and squeeze out as much liquid as possible. Add to the bowl containing the crabmeat. Add the mayonnaise, mustard, and 1 cup bread crumbs and mix well. If the mixture seems too wet to shape, add more bread crumbs. Season with salt and pepper.

To stuff the fillets, rinse the fish under cold running water and pat dry with paper towels. Run your fingertips along the flesh to make sure all of the bones have been removed. Lay a fillet flat on a work surface. Place 1/4 cup of the crabmeat stuffing in the middle of the fillet, roll it up, and place seam side down in the prepared baking dish. Repeat with the remaining fillets and stuffing. Sprinkle the rolled fillets with salt, pepper, and paprika.

Place in the oven and bake for 20 to 25 minutes, until the flesh flakes when pressed gently with a fork. Do not overbake. Place each rolled fillet on a warmed dinner plate and serve immediately.

Lenten Macaroni and Cheese *(see photo insert)*

SERVES 4 TO 6

This favorite meatless dish is always a welcome change to the usual Friday-evening fish. It is so fast and easy to prepare that you will be shocked at how good it tastes. My mother used to bake her macaroni and cheese in a large Pyrex bowl, so each serving was hot and creamy.

1 pound elbow macaroni
2 tablespoons unsalted butter
1 large yellow onion, chopped
1 clove garlic, minced
2 (8-ounce) cans tomato sauce
1 pound Cheddar cheese, cubed

Preheat the oven to 350°. Grease a 2-quart ovenproof glass bowl or a 9 by 13-inch baking dish with butter. Bring a large pot of salted water to a boil over high heat. Add the macaroni and cook according to the package directions, until al dente.

Meanwhile, in a sauté pan, melt the butter over medium heat. Add the onion and garlic and sauté for 6 to 8 minutes, until golden brown and soft. Remove from the heat.

When the pasta is ready, drain and place in a large bowl. Add the onion and garlic and mix well. Add the tomato sauce and mix again. Add the cheese and stir until well incorporated. Pour into the prepared bowl.

Cover the bowl with aluminum foil and bake for 30 minutes, until hot and bubbly. Serve immediately, directly from the dish.

Chilled Broccoli with Lemon

SERVES 4 TO 6

If you like broccoli, buy extra, because this recipe is addictive. Somewhere along the way, cold vegetables and hot food became a no-no. I think when paired with a heavier entrée, the light crispness of the broccoli brings out all of the other flavors.

2 (1-pound) heads broccoli, trimmed into florets
Olive oil
Juice of 2 lemons
Salt
Freshly ground black pepper

Bring a large pot of salted water to a boil over high heat. Half-fill a large bowl with ice and add enough water to moisten the cubes.

Add the broccoli to the boiling water. Cook for 2 to 3 minutes, until crisp-tender. Drain and immediately place in the bowl of ice water to halt the cooking. Drain again and place on a large serving platter.

Drizzle the broccoli with the olive oil and lemon juice. Season with salt and pepper and serve.

Stuffed Tomatoes *(see photo insert)*

SERVES 4 TO 6

Everyone knows the sorry state of tomatoes in March. They remind us of small orange baseballs. These hothouse tomatoes offer one plus, however: they are great for stuffing and roasting in the oven. By the time March rolls around, everyone at the convent is so sick of frozen vegetables that this fresh side dish takes on an added glow.

1/4 cup pine nuts
4 tomatoes
Salt
Freshly ground black pepper
1 cup seasoned bread crumbs
1/4 cup grated Romano cheese
1 tablespoon chopped fresh parsley
2 tablespoons extra virgin olive oil

Preheat the oven to 350°. Spread the pine nuts on a small baking sheet in a single layer. Place in the oven and toast for 8 to 10 minutes, until golden brown. Remove from the oven and pour onto a plate to cool.

Increase the oven temperature to 375°. Line a baking sheet with aluminum foil and grease lightly with olive oil. Cut the tomatoes in half crosswise. If necessary, remove a thin slice from the bottom of each half to level the tomatoes. Place the tomato halves, cut sides up, on the baking sheet. With a melon baller or tea-spoon, scoop out some of the tomato pulp to allow room for the stuffing. Season with salt and pepper and set aside.

To prepare the stuffing, in a large bowl, combine the pine nuts, bread crumbs, cheese, and parsley. Toss until well blended. Add the oil and toss well. The mixture should hold together firmly when pressed in the palm of your hand. If the stuffing is too dry, add 1 to 2 tablespoons water until it holds together. Scoop the filling into the tomato halves, dividing evenly and pressing firmly as you create a mound.

Place in the oven and bake for 15 minutes, until the stuffing is golden brown and crusty. Remove from the oven and transfer to a serving platter. Serve while still hot and bubbly.

You have crowned the year with your bounty,
and your paths overflow with a rich harvest.

—Psalms 65:12

Tricolored Scones

MAKES 2 DOZEN

In honor of Saint Paddy's Day, I must include a recipe for traditional Irish buns, or, as most people know them, scones. They are great for breakfast or with your afternoon tea, and the Sisters often have them as a special treat with butter and jam.

5$1/2$ cups flour
1 cup sugar
4 teaspoons baking powder
1 teaspoon salt
1$1/2$ cups chilled unsalted butter
2 cups milk
$1/2$ cup dark raisins
$1/2$ cup golden raisins
$1/2$ cup dried cranberries

Preheat the oven to 425°. Have ready an ungreased baking sheet.

In a large bowl, whisk together the flour, sugar, baking powder, and salt. With a pastry blender or 2 butter knives, cut the butter into the dry ingredients until the mixture has the consistency of rolled oats. Add the milk and stir with a wooden spoon until a smooth dough forms. Stir in the raisins and cranberries. With a tablespoon, drop small, rounded mounds of dough onto the baking sheet, spacing them about 3 inches apart.

Place in the oven and bake for 15 to 20 minutes, until golden brown. Remove from the oven and serve immediately.

The Rule of Saint Benedict comes from the teachings of Saint Benedict, a man born in 480 A.D. in Nursia, a town thirty miles outside of Rome. There, as a student, he sampled the decadent and immoral life that sixth-century Rome had to offer and soon left the city to pursue the life of a hermit. When others heard of him and his way of life, they convinced him that his gift of prayer and reflection should be shared, and from here the monastic life was born.

The Rule of Saint Benedict is not a series of commands that must be followed to the letter, but a list of subjects that, when studied and put into daily life, becomes a way to live in the light of Christ's teachings. In the Rule, Saint Benedict talks of ways to serve meals, and I follow them as closely as I can. He speaks of offering more than one entrée, so that each in the community will be happy at mealtime. I also offer two vegetables and a starch, to appeal to all members.

While the constitutions of the Holy Rule were revised and updated in 1964, their basic tenets remain the same: Treat others with the care and respect that you would desire for yourself. Respect compassion and kindness and show hospitality whenever possible. These beliefs hold as true today as they did more than fifteen hundred years ago when Saint Benedict first offered them.

✠ *Saint Benedict and his sister, Saint Scholastica, flank the seal of Benedict, which welcomes visitors to Saint Walburga Monastery.*

APRIL

There is much to look forward to in the month of April. While it usually starts out cold and rainy, the showers truly do bring the May flowers. The convent grounds bloom with forsythia, and all of the Easter flowers begin poking their heads out of the freshly thawed earth. Daffodils, brightly colored tulips, and hyacinths abound.

Activity heightens around the convent as Easter approaches. The church is cleaned from top to bottom and fresh flowers are placed nearly everywhere. The windows and doors are opened to let in the warm spring breezes and chase out any remaining evidence of winter's chill. Easter is the most important day in the Catholic calendar, the feast day on which we celebrate the death and resurrection of Jesus Christ. It is a wonderful time of renewal and of remembering just why we do what we do the rest of the year.

In the kitchen, I find myself using foods that remind me of the season and all that is new around us. Lettuce greens that are picked just as they are reaching maturity, thin and delicate spears of asparagus, plus all of the fresh fruits and berries that are beginning to show up are as welcome as the sun.

April also has very special meanings for me. I chose the Easter season for my wedding, as I love this time of the year when the warmth of the sun feels so new on your face and you realize how lucky you are to be here to experience it. Other springtime gifts include my three children, who were all born around Easter. They have given my husband and me tangible examples of how special new life is and how we can all start fresh at this time of the year.

Baby Greens with a Raspberry Vinaigrette

SERVES 4 TO 6

In the interest of speed and efficiency, I am a firm believer in using products that save time and reduce work. Most local supermarkets now carry prepackaged mixed baby greens in the produce section. Using these prepped greens leaves you extra time to make a fabulous dressing that stars raspberries and fresh tarragon.

2 (12-ounce) packages mixed baby greens
1 bunch fresh tarragon

DRESSING
1/4 cup sugar, or as needed
2 pints fresh raspberries, or 1 (10-ounce) bag frozen raspberries, thawed
1/4 cup tarragon-flavored vinegar
2 tablespoons Dijon mustard
1/2 cup olive oil
Salt
Freshly ground black pepper

1/2 cup thinly sliced red onion
1/2 cup chopped walnuts
1 pear, peeled, cored, and chopped
1 pint fresh raspberries, for garnish

Rinse the greens thoroughly in a large amount of water, then drain and dry in a lettuce spinner. Transfer to a large salad bowl, cover with a damp paper towel, and place in the refrigerator until ready to serve. Pick the tarragon leaves off the stems, rinse, and dry in the lettuce spinner. Reserving 2 tablespoons whole leaves for garnish, chop the remaining tarragon.

To prepare the dressing, combine the 1/4 cup sugar and raspberries in a food processor or blender and process until puréed. To remove the seeds, pass through a fine-mesh sieve placed over a bowl, using a spoon or ladle to push the purée against the sieve to make the messy job easier. Add the chopped tarragon, vinegar, and mustard to the purée and mix well. Whisk in the olive oil briskly. Taste and, if the raspberries are a little tart, add a bit more sugar. Season with salt and pepper.

Remove the greens from the refrigerator and add the onion, walnuts, and pear. Toss with the dressing and garnish with the whole raspberries and reserved tarragon leaves. Serve immediately.

Let us at least agree to drink modestly and not to the point of excess, for "wine makes even the wise go astray" (Sirach 19:2).

—The Rule of Saint Benedict, chapter 40

Asparagus with the Fastest Hollandaise in the East

SERVES 4 TO 6   *(see photo insert)*

For several years, I didn't make hollandaise sauce for the Sisters because I was haunted by the memory of making sixty-egg batches in restaurants. I can still feel the cramps in my hands and arms from all the whisking. Sometimes the sauce would break, or separate, and I would have to start all over again. This recipe is made in the food processor, so you can save your aching back.

1 pound thin asparagus

HOLLANDAISE SAUCE
1/2 cup plus 2 tablespoons unsalted butter
4 egg yolks
2 tablespoons freshly squeezed lemon juice
1/4 teaspoon salt
1/4 teaspoon freshly ground black pepper
Hot-pepper sauce

To prepare the asparagus, break off the tough ends of the spears. Bring a large pot of water to a boil over high heat. Place the asparagus in the boiling water and cook for 3 to 5 minutes, until bright green and still crunchy. Drain, place on a warmed serving platter, and cover loosely to keep warm.

To prepare the sauce, in a small saucepan over low heat, melt the butter until bubbling. Swirl constantly to avoid browning. In a food processor or blender, combine the egg yolks, lemon juice, salt, and pepper. Process for about 30 seconds. With the motor on low speed, slowly add the hot butter. Do not overmix, or the sauce will break. Add pepper sauce to taste and adjust the seasoning as necessary.

Drain off any accumulated liquid from the asparagus. Drizzle the sauce over the spears and serve immediately.

Roast Leg of Lamb with Lemon and Garlic

SERVES 6 TO 8

This recipe comes in handy in April, as leg of lamb is a staple on many Easter and Passover tables. When I first started cooking for the Sisters, most of them did not care for the relatively strong flavor of lamb, but they've come around, partly due to this dish. Here, I have included a marinade that reduces that intensity while tenderizing the meat at the same time.

1 (3- to 4-pound) boned leg of lamb, tied
2 cups olive oil
1 cup freshly squeezed lemon juice
1 tablespoon salt
2 teaspoons freshly ground black pepper
1 tablespoon garlic powder
1 teaspoon paprika
3 bay leaves
2 carrots, peeled and cut into thirds
2 celery stalks, cut into thirds
1 yellow onion, quartered
1 cup water

Rinse the lamb under cold running water and pat dry with paper towels. To prepare the marinade, in a small bowl, combine the olive oil, lemon juice, salt, pepper, garlic powder, paprika, and bay leaves. Place the lamb in a large resealable plastic bag. Pour the marinade over the lamb. Roll the top of the bag down to expel as much air as possible before sealing. Massage the marinade into the meat to coat evenly. Place the bag in a large roasting pan and refrigerate for at least 3 hours, or preferably overnight. Turn the bag several times to redistribute the marinade.

(continued)

Preheat the oven to 425°. Place the carrots, celery, and onion in the bottom of a large roasting pan. (They will prevent the roast from sticking to the pan as well as make the pan juices delicious for gravy.) Remove the lamb from the bag and place on top of the vegetables. Discard the bag and marinade.

Place in the oven and roast for 20 minutes. Decrease the temperature to 350° and continue to roast for about 1 hour, until it reaches an internal temperature of 165° for medium. Remove from the oven, transfer the roast to a warmed large platter, and tent loosely with aluminum foil. Allow to rest for at least 20 minutes before slicing.

Scrape the pan drippings and vegetables into a saucepan. Spoon off as much fat as possible. Place the roasting pan on the stovetop over low heat. Add the water and deglaze the pan, scraping up any brown bits with a wooden spatula. Add this liquid to the saucepan with the vegetables. Place the saucepan over high heat and bring to a boil. Pass through a fine-mesh sieve into a warmed gravy boat or bowl, discarding the solids. Taste and adjust the seasoning with salt and pepper if necessary.

Slice the roast into 1/4-inch-thick slices and place on the platter. Serve with the gravy on the side.

Poached Salmon with Mirepoix and Dijonnaise Sauce *(see photo insert)*

SERVES 6

If you are looking for a visually appealing entrée to replace the same old ham or turkey on your holiday table, this easy recipe will produce a delicious and attractive dish. When I prepare it for the Sisters, I use a whole side of salmon. It serves ten people and makes for a beautiful presentation.

SAUCE
1 cup mayonnaise
1/4 cup Dijon mustard
1 tablespoon dried dill

6 (4-ounce) salmon fillets
1 cup dry white wine
1 cup fish stock (page 200), or 1 (8-ounce) bottle clam juice
Garlic salt
Freshly ground black pepper
1 bunch fresh dill
1 yellow onion, chopped
4 celery stalks, julienned
3 carrots, peeled and julienned
Lemon wedges, for garnish

To prepare the sauce, in a bowl, combine the mayonnaise, mustard, and dried dill. Cover and place in the refrigerator.

To prepare the salmon, preheat the oven to 350°. Evenly grease the bottom of a large glass or ceramic baking dish with butter. Run your fingertips along the salmon flesh to make sure all of the bones have been removed. Place the salmon in the dish and pour over the wine and stock. Dust the salmon with the garlic salt and pepper, and top with several sprigs of the dill. Reserve the remaining dill for garnish. Sprinkle the onion, celery, and carrots over the salmon to cover generously. Cover the pan tightly with aluminum foil.

Bake the salmon for 15 to 20 minutes, until the flesh flakes when pressed gently with a fork. Do not overbake. It will continue to cook after it is removed from the oven.

Transfer the salmon to a serving platter. With a slotted spoon, lift the vegetables out of the cooking liquid and mound on top of the salmon. Garnish with lemon wedges and the reserved dill sprigs. Serve hot or chilled with the mustard sauce on the side.

Roast Pork Loin with Olives and Capers (page 12) and Whipped Potatoes (page 16)

Poached Salmon with Mirepoix and Dijonnaise Sauce (page 61) and Asparagus with the Fastest Hollandaise in the East (page 58)

Lenten Macaroni and Cheese (page 48) and Stuffed Tomatoes (page 50)

Cut-It-Out Sugar Cookies (page 33)

Chicken Breasts with Ham and Peas

SERVES 6

I always keep boneless chicken breasts in the freezer in case of a sudden menu change due to unexpected guests. On many days, one of the Sisters will come to tell me to expect an extra ten or fifteen people at dinner that evening. This recipe can be thrown together in a flash and is a guaranteed crowd pleaser.

2 pounds boneless, skinless chicken breasts
1 cup flour
1 teaspoon salt
1 teaspoon freshly ground black pepper
1 teaspoon garlic powder
1 teaspoon paprika
2 tablespoons vegetable oil
1 small yellow onion, chopped
1 cup chopped deli-style smoked ham
1 cup dry white wine
2 cups half-and-half or light cream
1 cup frozen petite peas, thawed
1/2 cup grated Romano cheese
1 bunch fresh parsley, chopped
1 pound dried wide egg noodles

Rinse the chicken under cold running water and pat dry with paper towels. Trim off and discard any visible fat and cut the breasts into thin slices. On a sheet of waxed paper, mix together the flour, salt, pepper, garlic powder, and paprika. Dredge the chicken in the flour mixture and shake off the excess. Separate any slices that stick together.

(continued)

Place a large sauté pan over high heat and add the oil. When it is very hot, add the chicken in an even layer. Sauté for about 6 minutes, until golden brown on all sides. Remove from the pan and keep warm. Add the onion to the pan and sauté for 4 minutes, until soft. Add the ham and sauté for 4 minutes, until warmed. Add the wine and deglaze the pan, scraping up any brown bits with a wooden spatula. Bring to a boil and cook for 8 to 10 minutes, until reduced by half. Add the half-and-half and peas. Return to a boil, then decrease the heat to medium. Simmer, stirring occasionally, for about 8 minutes, until slightly thickened and the cream loses its raw flavor.

Add the cheese and stir until melted. Add 1/4 cup of the chopped parsley, reserving the remainder for garnish. Taste and adjust the seasoning if necessary. Return the chicken to the pan and simmer for 5 minutes.

About 15 minutes before the chicken is ready, bring a large pot of salted water to a boil over high heat. Add the noodles and cook according to the package instructions, until al dente. Drain and divide evenly among 6 warmed dinner plates. Spoon the chicken and sauce over the top, again dividing evenly. Garnish with the reserved chopped parsley and serve immediately.

Classic Cheese Soufflé

SERVES 4 TO 6

Making a soufflé sounds too daunting to many cooks. The vision of lots of hard work being destroyed because someone makes a loud noise or opens the oven at the wrong time is a common misconception. This recipe is very easy—it has to be in order to make it for sixty people. Served with a bowl of homemade soup and toasted French bread, the soufflé is one of the Sisters' favorite Friday-evening meals.

1/4 cup unsalted butter
1/4 cup flour
1 teaspoon salt
1/2 teaspoon freshly ground black pepper
1/2 teaspoon garlic powder
1 1/2 cups milk
2 cups shredded Cheddar cheese
6 eggs, separated

Preheat the oven to 350°. Grease the bottom of a 2-quart soufflé dish with butter. Do not grease the sides, as the soufflé needs to grab onto them to rise.

In a saucepan over medium heat, melt the butter. Stir in the flour, salt, pepper, and garlic powder and cook, stirring constantly, for 2 minutes, until golden brown. (This is a roux.) Remove from the heat and whisk in the milk until smooth. Return to medium heat and simmer, stirring frequently, for 10 minutes, until smooth and creamy. Add the cheese and stir until incorporated. Remove from the heat.

With an electric mixer on high speed, whip the egg whites until they hold a peak but are not dry. In another bowl, whisk the egg yolks until pale yellow.

(continued)

Stir a spoonful of the hot cheese sauce into the yolks to temper them and to prevent them from curdling. Slowly add a little more of the hot sauce to the yolks until they are warm, then whisk the yolk mixture back into the cheese sauce. Transfer the yolk mixture to a large bowl.

Carefully fold about one-fourth of the egg whites into the yolk mixture to lighten the yolks. Add the remaining whites and gently fold until no white streaks remain. Pour into the prepared soufflé dish. With a paring knife, score a circle around the top of the batter about 3 inches from the rim of the dish. This will allow a crown to form.

Bake for 35 minutes, until tall and golden brown. Do not open the oven during cooking, as the change in temperature will cause the soufflé to fall. Serve immediately.

Carrot and Pineapple Cake with Cream Cheese Frosting

SERVES 10

When my husband and I decided to get married, I naturally wanted to be very involved in planning the menu for our reception. I had always dreamed of a multi-tiered wedding cake that featured a different flavor and texture in each tier so that everyone would be satisfied, and that's what we had. The bottom tier was by far the most popular. It was a carrot cake, thick with pineapple and walnuts, then filled and iced with a cream cheese frosting. Quite a few of the nuns loved it, and it is still requested several times a year for large feast days and special occasions. For an extra-special treat, I sometimes decorate the sides of the cake with chopped walnuts and pipe orange- and green-tinted frosting into carrots on the top.

2 cups flour
1 teaspoon baking soda
1/2 teaspoon salt
2 teaspoons ground cinnamon
1 1/2 cups vegetable oil
2 cups granulated sugar
3 eggs
1 teaspoon pure vanilla extract
2 cups finely grated carrot
1 cup drained crushed pineapple
1 cup chopped walnuts
1 cup sweetened flaked coconut

FROSTING
1 (8-ounce) package cream cheese, at room temperature
1/2 cup unsalted butter, at room temperature
2 teaspoons pure vanilla extract
4 cups confectioners' sugar, sifted

Preheat the oven to 350°. Grease and flour 3 round cake pans, each 9 inches in diameter.

To prepare the cake, sift together the flour, baking soda, salt, and cinnamon into a bowl. In a large bowl, with an electric mixer on high speed, beat together the oil and granulated sugar until light and fluffy. Add the eggs one at a time and whip until pale yellow. Add the vanilla and mix well. Add the carrot, pineapple, walnuts, and coconut and mix with a wooden spoon until well incorporated.

With the spoon, fold the flour mixture into the carrot mixture. Mix gently to avoid toughening the batter. Divide the batter evenly among the 3 prepared pans.

Bake the cake for 25 to 30 minutes, until a toothpick inserted into the center comes out clean. Allow to cool for 10 minutes in the pans on cooling racks and then invert onto the racks to cool completely. (The layers can be frozen for up to 2 weeks for later assembly. Thaw overnight in the refrigerator before continuing.)

To prepare the frosting, in a large bowl, combine the cream cheese and butter. With an electric mixer on high speed, cream together until light and fluffy. Beat in the vanilla. Slowly add the confectioners' sugar and continue to whip until smooth and airy. If the frosting seems too soft to spread, cover and place in the refrigerator for 10 minutes, then mix by hand to achieve the desired consistency.

To assemble the cake, place 1 cake layer on an attractive serving plate. Spread one-quarter of the frosting over the top. Top with another layer and repeat with another one-quarter of the frosting. Top with the third layer and use the remaining frosting to cover the top and sides of the cake generously. Serve immediately or place in the refrigerator until ready to serve.

A primary focus of the Benedictine order is the importance of education. The Sisters guide the educational program for four schools in the area. Across the street from the Motherhouse is the Benedictine Academy, a secondary school that caters solely to young women and is known for having produced many strong professionals now working in communities both far and near.

The Sisters also run two elementary schools that serve the surrounding community, both of which offer, in the Benedictine tradition, a solid curriculum that prepares students for the future. The children receive an education based on the fundamentals of the Catholic religion—fundamentals that stress a positive Christian way of life. The Sisters' fourth school is the Benedictine Preschool, which my own children have attended. The three- and four-year-olds are kept busy learning their ABCs and 123s, as well as science and religion, all the while having access to everything that the convent grounds have to offer. Visiting the church and infirmary have become enriching experiences for the children as well as for the Sisters.

✠ *The Sisters' high school, Benedictine Academy.*

MAY

On Mother's Day, it's nice to encourage mothers to stay out of the kitchen and take the day off. Breakfast in bed or a fancy brunch at home or at a restaurant are traditional ways to pamper mothers on their special day, so I have included some tasty dishes that would be perfect for a breakfast tray or a midmorning brunch.

At the convent, we celebrate Mary, the mother of Jesus. On May Day, a celebration is always held during which the statue of the Blessed Mother is crowned with fresh flowers and schoolchildren sing songs in honor of her life and its influence on the Church. These inaugural days of May also bring the first hints of summer to the convent. The end of the school year is quickly approaching, and the Sisters begin to make their summer vacation plans. The days become warmer, while the nights still cling to the damp chill of spring. We usually get at least one or two ninety-degree days, which wake us up to the fact that summer is just around the corner and we had better get ready. Flower and vegetable gardens are planned, and the menu adjusts accordingly.

As the weather heats up, the meals begin to get lighter as I move toward more fish and chicken dishes. The produce is improving by leaps and bounds, so I add more and more fresh fruits and vegetables. While the locally grown favorites are just beginning their growing season, such standards as tomatoes, sweet corn, and green beans come in daily from Florida and California. I find that the Sisters appreciate simple, yet satisfying main courses like Quick Quiche and Zucchini Torte this time of year. These dishes also freeze and travel well, making them easy to tote to Memorial Day outings.

Salade Niçoise

SERVES 6 TO 8

This traditional French salad is a meal in itself. Paired with a couple of hot, crunchy baguettes, it makes a great lunch for any special mom. The Sisters especially like the lemon-garlic dressing, which, while common in other parts of the world, came as a surprise to them. A salad dressing that didn't use mayonnaise or vinegar was a nice alternative to the creamy Italian or Thousand Island that had been the previous standards. The secret to this recipe is readying all ingredients before beginning to assemble the salad.

1 pound green beans, ends trimmed
2 pounds baby Red Bliss potatoes
1/4 cup olive oil
1/4 cup red wine vinegar
1 teaspoon salt
1/2 teaspoon freshly ground black pepper
1 tablespoon chopped fresh tarragon, or 1/2 teaspoon dried tarragon
1 head romaine lettuce
2 heads Boston lettuce
1 (3-ounce) can albacore tuna packed in olive oil
1 lemon, halved
4 hard-boiled eggs
1 cucumber, peeled and sliced
1 red onion, thinly sliced
4 ripe plum tomatoes, chopped
1 cup pitted black olives
10 anchovy fillets

DRESSING
1/2 cup freshly squeezed lemon juice
2 cloves garlic
1/4 cup chopped fresh parsley
2 teaspoons salt
1 teaspoon freshly ground black pepper
1 cup olive oil

Bring a large pot of salted water to a boil over high heat. Add the green beans and cook for 3 to 4 minutes, until bright green and crisp-tender. Remove from the water with a slotted spoon and rinse with cold water to halt the cooking. Place in a bowl, cover, and refrigerate.

To the still boiling water, add the potatoes and decrease the heat to medium. Cook for 10 to 15 minutes, until fork tender. Drain and place in a bowl. Toss with the olive oil, vinegar, salt, pepper, and tarragon. Cover and refrigerate.

Tear all the lettuce into bite-sized pieces. Rinse thoroughly in a large amount of water, drain, and dry in a lettuce spinner. Arrange the lettuce on the biggest round platter you have. Cover with damp paper towels and refrigerate.

Place the tuna in a bowl. Squeeze the lemon over it. Toss well and season with salt and pepper. Cover and refrigerate. Peel and rinse the eggs, then cut in half lengthwise. Place on a small plate, cover, and refrigerate.

To assemble the salad, remove all the ingredients from the refrigerator. Mound the tuna in the center of the lettuce. Arrange the green beans around the tuna, radiating them outward like wheel spokes. Between the spokes, make more spokes with the potatoes. Arrange the egg halves, cut side up, around the edge of the lettuce. Fill in the empty spaces with the cucumber, onion, tomatoes, and olives. Make an X across the top of the tuna with the anchovies, and garnish the eggs with the anchovies overlapped like ribbons. Cover the salad with damp paper towels and chill until ready to serve.

To prepare the dressing, in a food processor, combine the lemon juice, garlic, parsley, salt, and pepper. Pulse until well blended. Scrape down the sides of the bowl. With the motor on low speed, add the oil in a slow, steady stream until emulsified. Pour into a bowl, taste, and adjust the seasoning if necessary. Drizzle enough dressing over the salad to coat lightly. Serve each guest a little of each ingredient and offer the extra dressing on the side.

Quick Quiche *(see photo insert)*

SERVES 6

Quiche is one of those dishes that seems to make cooks nervous. Once you learn the secret of a good custard, the rest is a snap. While I usually serve quiche on Fridays as a meatless meal, nearly any cooked meat or seafood can be added to the egg mixture. I have used grilled chicken, sausage, ham, crabmeat, shrimp, and, of course, the traditional bacon found in quiche Lorraine. I think that a mix of one meat, one cheese, and various vegetables makes the best-tasting quiche, so get out your favorites. When time is tight, I have found that today's frozen pie crusts are such good products that they make a fine substitute to making your own.

1/2 recipe pie crust (page 202), or 1 (9-inch) frozen deep-dish pie crust

2 cups half-and-half

4 eggs

1 teaspoon salt

1/2 teaspoon freshly ground black pepper

1/4 teaspoon ground nutmeg

1/2 cup chopped cooked meat or seafood, such as bacon, ham, chicken, or sausage or smoked salmon

1/2 cup shredded or crumbled cheese, such as Swiss, Cheddar, mozzarella, provolone, feta, or chèvre

1/2 cup sautéed or steamed diced vegetables, such as onions, bell peppers, tomatoes, broccoli, and mushrooms, in any combination

Preheat the oven to 350°. Line a baking sheet with aluminum foil. If making your own pie crust, follow the directions in the pie crust recipe to roll out the dough and line a 9-inch deep-dish pie pan. Place the pie crust on the baking sheet.

(continued)

In a bowl, whisk together the half-and-half, eggs, salt, pepper, and nutmeg until frothy and pale yellow. Sprinkle the meat in the bottom of the pie crust. Sprinkle the cheese over the meat. Sprinkle the vegetables over the cheese and meat. Slowly pour the egg mixture over the top.

Place in the oven and bake for 35 to 45 minutes, until puffy and golden brown. Remove from the oven and allow to cool for 10 minutes. Cut into 6 wedges and serve at once.

First and foremost, thee must be no word or sign of the evil
of grumbling, no manifestation of it for any reason at all.
If, however, anyone is caught grumbling, let them undergo
more severe discipline.

—The Rule of Saint Benedict, chapter 34

Lemon Chicken

SERVES 6

Whenever a major feast day or an anniversary jubilee is celebrated, the Sisters like to see this dish on the menu because it is light and tasty and the majority of guests enjoy it. On one such occasion, I made it for 275 people. Now, that's a lot of chicken!

6 boneless chicken breast halves, skin on, trimmed of excess fat
1/2 cup flour
2 teaspoons salt
1 teaspoon freshly ground black pepper
1 teaspoon garlic powder
1 teaspoon paprika
1/4 cup olive oil
1 cup chicken stock (page 197)
1/4 cup freshly squeezed lemon juice
2 tablespoons chopped fresh parsley, plus extra for garnish
Lemon slices, for garnish

Rinse the chicken under cold running water and pat dry with paper towels. One at a time, place the chicken breasts between 2 sheets of plastic wrap. Using a meat mallet, carefully pound the breasts to a uniform thickness of about 1/2 inch. On a separate sheet of plastic wrap, combine the flour, salt, pepper, garlic powder, and paprika.

Place a large sauté pan over high heat and add the oil. When the oil is hot, dredge the chicken breasts in the flour mixture and shake off any excess. Place in the hot pan and brown, turning once, for 3 to 4 minutes on each side, until golden brown on the outside and cooked through and no longer pink on the inside. Remove from the pan, place on a warmed large platter, and cover loosely to keep warm.

(continued)

Return the pan to high heat, add the stock, and deglaze the pan, scraping up any brown bits with a wooden spatula. Simmer to reduce the stock by one-third, about 12 minutes. Add the lemon juice and season with salt, pepper, and the 2 tablespoons parsley.

To serve, place 1 chicken breast on each of 6 warmed dinner plates. Drizzle 2 tablespoons of sauce over each serving. Garnish with lemon slices and the remaining chopped parsley.

Stuffed Meat Loaf Cordon Bleu

SERVES 4 TO 6

Meat loaf is the queen of the traditional American menu. People have tried beef, pork, veal, chicken, turkey, and even tofu in various combinations, but I think this recipe, calling for beef and ham, rules. The addition of the salty, sweet ham and chewy mozzarella cheese makes it an entrée worthy of any Mother's Day table. That assessment is particularly fitting, as my mother was the creator of this particular recipe. Any leftovers will gladly be snatched up for meat loaf sandwiches for the next day's lunch.

1 pound ground beef
1 egg
1 teaspoon salt
1/2 teaspoon freshly ground black pepper
1 teaspoon garlic powder
1 tablespoon chopped fresh oregano, or 1 teaspoon dried oregano
1 cup milk
1 to 2 cups seasoned bread crumbs
6 to 9 slices smoked and sugar-cured ham, not too thin
6 to 9 slices mozzarella cheese, not too thin

Preheat the oven to 350°. Line a large baking sheet with aluminum foil and grease with vegetable oil.

In a large bowl, mix together the ground beef, egg, salt, pepper, garlic powder, oregano, and milk. Add 1 cup of the bread crumbs and mix well. If the mixture seems too wet, add more bread crumbs as needed until the mixture is smooth and holds together when squeezed in the palm of your hand.

Lay a 12 by 18-inch sheet of plastic wrap on a work surface. Place the meat mixture in the center of the plastic wrap and start working it out to the corners. You want to create a uniform thickness, with no holes, that reaches to the edges of the plastic. Lay the ham slices on top of the meat mixture, covering it uniformly and leaving a 2-inch border of meat around the edge to aid in sealing the roll. In the same way, lay the cheese slices on top of the ham, maintaining the 2-inch border.

Grasping the plastic wrap, fold the 2-inch borders on the right and left edges over the ham and cheese. Holding the plastic wrap firmly at the edge closest to you, start rolling up the meat. As you go, squish and mold the roll to force out as much air as possible. When you get to the last turn, roll it back toward you and pinch the seal closed. Pick up the whole thing and roll it off the plastic wrap onto the prepared baking sheet, resting it seam side down to avoid losing any of the good insides during cooking.

Bake for 45 minutes, until browned and bubbly. Remove from the oven, tent loosely with aluminum foil, and let rest for 20 minutes. To serve, slice the loaf into 2-inch-thick slices and place 2 slices on each dinner plate.

Zucchini Torte

SERVES 4 TO 8

When planning a special brunch, I love to include recipes that create wonderful taste and texture combinations. This recipe does just that, as well as being tasty served hot or at room temperature. It also makes a great hors d'oeuvre when cut into bite-sized squares and is lovely served garnished with fresh fruit.

4 tablespoons chilled unsalted butter
1 yellow onion, chopped
1 clove garlic, minced
2 cups flour
1 teaspoon salt
1 tablespoon baking powder
3 tablespoons chilled high-quality vegetable shortening
1 cup milk
3 eggs
2 pounds zucchini, quartered lengthwise and thinly sliced
1 pound Cheddar cheese, shredded
1 tablespoon chopped fresh basil, or 1/2 teaspoon dried basil
1 tablespoon chopped fresh thyme, or 1/2 teaspoon dried thyme
1 tablespoon chopped fresh rosemary, or 1/2 teaspoon dried rosemary

Preheat the oven to 350°. Grease a 9 by 13-inch glass or ceramic baking dish with vegetable oil.

In a small sauté pan over medium heat, melt 1 tablespoon of the butter. Add the onion and garlic and sauté for 8 minutes, until the onion softens. Remove from the heat and allow to cool.

In a large bowl, combine the flour, salt, and baking powder and stir together with a fork. Using a pastry blender or 2 butter knives, cut the remaining 3 tablespoons butter and the shortening into the dry ingredients until the mixture has the consistency of rolled oats. Add the milk and eggs and whisk together until well incorporated. Add the onion-garlic mixture, zucchini, cheese, basil, thyme, and rosemary. Stir until well incorporated. Pour into the prepared baking dish.

Bake for 35 to 45 minutes, until golden brown and slightly puffy. Remove from the oven and let cool for 10 minutes before serving, or let cool completely and serve at room temperature. To serve as an hors d'ocuvre, cut into 1-inch squares. To serve as a side dish, cut into 4-inch squares. To serve as an entrée, cut into 4 by 6-inch rectangles.

Fresh Veggie Stew

SERVES 6 TO 8

The Sisters love this recipe when I turn it into an entrée with the addition of chunks of fresh mozzarella, tossing them in at the last minute and then continuing to cook until they just begin to melt. It is also nice prepared without the cheese and served as a side dish to accompany a less complicated entrée such as Quick Quiche (page 75). It goes great with hot Italian bread, too.

1 (2-ounce) jar oil-packed sundried tomatoes, drained, with oil reserved,
    and chopped
4 cloves garlic, chopped
1 large yellow onion, chopped
1 large green bell pepper, stemmed, seeded, and chopped
1 large red bell pepper, stemmed, seeded, and chopped
1 pound yellow squashes, quartered lengthwise and chopped
1 pound zucchini, quartered lengthwise and chopped
2 (28-ounce) cans Italian-style diced tomatoes
2 (16-ounce) cans pitted small black olives, drained and chopped
1/2 cup grated Romano cheese, plus extra for garnish
1 pound fresh mozzarella cheese in water, cut into large cubes
1 bunch fresh basil, chopped
Salt
Freshly ground black pepper

Place a large pot over high heat. Add the sundried tomatoes along with their oil and the garlic and sauté for 1 minute, until the garlic is aromatic. Add the onion, red and green bell peppers, yellow squashes, and zucchini and stir to coat with the oil. Cover, decrease the heat to medium-high, and allow the vegetables to sweat for 8 to 10 minutes, until fork tender.

(continued)

Stir in the tomatoes and olives, decrease the heat to medium, and simmer for 45 to 60 minutes, until the vegetables are soft and the flavors have melded. Add the 1/2 cup Romano cheese, the mozzarella cheese, and the basil. Decrease the heat to low and stir until the mozzarella begins to soften and melt. Taste and adjust the seasoning with salt and pepper if necessary.

To serve, ladle into soup bowls and sprinkle with additional Romano cheese.

A generous pound of bread is enough for a day whether for only one meal or for both dinner and supper.

—The Rule of Saint Benedict, chapter 39

Strawberry and Kiwi Pavlova

SERVES 6 TO 8

A Pavlova is a classic dessert using a baked meringue as a crust. Some of the Sisters have commented that the final creation resembles fruit on a cloud and tastes heavenly.

MERINGUE
4 egg whites
1¼ cups sugar
1 teaspoon pure vanilla extract
2 teaspoons cornstarch
1 teaspoon freshly squeezed lemon juice

2 cups heavy cream
¼ cup sugar
1 teaspoon pure vanilla extract
6 kiwis, peeled and thinly sliced, plus extra slices for garnish
2 pints fresh strawberries, hulled and thinly sliced, plus extra slices for garnish

Preheat the oven to 300°. Line 2 baking sheets with parchment paper. Using an 8-inch cake pan, trace 3 circles on the parchment paper.

To prepare the meringue, place the egg whites and sugar in a bowl. With an electric mixer on high speed, beat until soft peaks form. Add the vanilla, cornstarch, and lemon juice and continue to beat for 2 to 3 minutes, until thick and shiny. Divide the meringue among the 3 circles and spread evenly with a spatula, following the traced outlines on the paper.

Place the meringues in the oven and bake for 1 hour, until only slightly golden brown and a crust has formed on each, indicating that they are completely dry throughout. Remove from the oven and allow to cool completely on the baking sheets placed on cooling racks (do not remove from the sheets until completely cooled).

To prepare the filling, place the cream, sugar, and vanilla in a bowl. With an electric mixer on high speed, whip until soft peaks form. Carefully peel the meringues off the parchment paper. Place a meringue layer on a serving plate and spread one-third of the cream over it. Alternating kiwi and strawberry slices, layer one-third of the fruits over the cream. Place the second meringue over the fruit and repeat the process, using half of the remaining cream and fruits. Top with the third layer, cover the top with the remaining cream, and decorate with the remaining fruit. Refrigerate the cake for 20 minutes to soften before serving.

To serve, slice into wedges and garnish each serving with additional kiwi and strawberry slices.

Feast days have become an integral part of my menu planning. The Sisters do not celebrate their birthdays, but instead celebrate their chosen feast days. This is usually the day on the Catholic calendar that honors the saint from whom they have taken their Benedictine name. A good example would be Sister Patrick. Saint Patrick's feast day, as most people know, falls on March 17. Therefore, each March 17 is Sister Patrick's feast day.

On a Sister's feast day, she gets to choose anything she wants for dinner. This means she must tell me what she wants for the salad, the entrée, the starch, the two vegetables, and, of course, dessert. When I first started cooking for the Sisters, the menu choices ran to a simple baked chicken or roast beef. Once the community realized my culinary capabilities, their choices became more daring, with poached salmon or cheese soufflé frequent choices. Whether it's Sister Andrea's sauerbraten with dumplings or Sister Flavia's stuffed pork chops with apples and raisins, each feast day menu offers an individual challenge in the kitchen.

✠ *Sisters Lauren, Patrick, Mariette, and Marcia.*

JUNE

Many milestones are marked in the month of June: Father's Day, high school and college graduations, and, of course, all the June weddings. Around the convent, the Sisters are getting ready for their own summer schedules. The end of the school year is finally here, and most of the Sisters are busy preparing for it. Report cards and final exams bring the year to a climactic ending. Graduations are planned for the preschoolers, the kindergartners, the eighth graders, and, most importantly, for the high school seniors. The Sisters also take this time to recognize many of their alumni from ten, twenty-five, and even fifty years ago. Receptions and fund-raisers are organized and the month, with all of its events, just flies by.

June brings the Sisters' big retreat week, too. During this time, as many members of the community as possible gather for five days of silence, marked with special lectures by a guest speaker and different activities to refresh and renew their spiritual lives. For me, it means breakfast, lunch, and dinner for up to one hundred Sisters. By the end of the week, believe me, I need a silent retreat!

The convent grounds are beginning to bloom with summer annuals and vegetables are starting to show some real growth. A beautiful rose garden, tended by the Sisters for many generations, lies off the Gathering Space in the church. As June rolls around, the roses are just beginning to unfurl, and soon the bushes will be so heavy with brightly colored and beautifully scented flowers that they will loll over onto the sidewalks, creating pathways full of color and fragrance. A fountain in the center of the garden gurgles softly. Many come to pray and reflect at this spot, the resting place of the convent's founder, Mother Walburga.

In the kitchen, fresh fruits and vegetables become the stars of the menu. Some summers, I have tended a vegetable garden right outside my kitchen door. I planted deep red New Jersey beefsteak tomatoes, green beans, zucchini, and even basil for pesto. The sunny location is perfect for a garden. The terra-cotta brick walls keep the plants cool during the hot days of summer and warm through the chilly nights of September and early October, guaranteeing fresh produce well into the fall.

As the weather gets hotter, appetites often fade, so I try to keep meals cool and light. Occasionally, the Sisters prefer to have only a salad, so I serve one that fills all of their nutritional needs, such as the Seashell Salad. I find that tasty, uncomplicated entrées are popular this time of year, too. The Penne with Grilled Chicken in a Pink Tomato Sauce is a perfect example of that. Cauliflower with Seasoned Bread Crumbs is delicious hot or at room temperature, so try it the next time the weather seems just too hot and sticky for anyone to want to eat.

Seashell Salad

SERVES 6 TO 8

If the day is a real scorcher, this cool starter served on a bed of Boston lettuce is a delicious treat. In addition to being tasty and refreshing, it also contains a starch, a fruit, a protein, a vegetable, and a fat—a complete meal that is ready in a snap.

1 pound small shell pasta
1/4 cup pineapple juice
1 cup mayonnaise
2 tablespoons sugar
2 tablespoons fresh dill leaves, or 1 tablespoon dried dill, plus extra for garnish
1 pound high-quality crabmeat substitute
2 cups cubed fresh pineapple
4 celery stalks, thinly sliced crosswise
Salt
Freshly ground black pepper

Bring a large pot of salted water to a boil over high heat. Add the pasta and cook according to the package instructions, until al dente. Drain in a colander and rinse under cold water to cool. Shake and drain again.

To prepare the dressing, in a large bowl, combine the pineapple juice, mayonnaise, sugar, and dill and mix well.

To prepare the salad, add the cooled pasta to the dressing and toss. Chop the crab into bite-sized pieces. Add to the pasta and toss to distribute evenly. Add the pineapple and celery and toss well. Taste and adjust the seasoning with salt and pepper if necessary.

Toss well once again and garnish with dill, then serve.

Penne with Grilled Chicken in a Pink Tomato Sauce

SERVES 6 TO 8

This recipe started out as penne with vodka sauce. But the community asked for it so frequently that the Sister who does the shopping became embarrassed from having to buy so much vodka at the liquor store. After that, this "dry" version was born. If vine-ripened tomatoes can't be found, substitute a 28-ounce can of high-quality, Italian-style diced tomatoes.

MARINADE
1/2 cup extra virgin olive oil
1/2 cup red wine vinegar
1 tablespoon chopped green bell pepper
1 tablespoon chopped red bell pepper
1 clove garlic, minced
2 tablespoons chopped yellow onion
1 teaspoon salt
1/2 teaspoon freshly ground black pepper

1 pound boneless, skinless chicken breasts
1 pound penne pasta
2 tablespoons olive oil
1 yellow onion, chopped
2 cups half-and-half
3 cups peeled, seeded, and chopped fresh tomatoes
1 cup grated Romano cheese, plus extra for garnish
1 teaspoon freshly ground black pepper
3 tablespoons chopped fresh basil, plus extra for garnish
Salt

To prepare the marinade, combine the oil, vinegar, bell peppers, garlic, onion, salt, and pepper in a small bowl.

To marinate the chicken, place the breasts in a shallow baking dish. Pour the marinade over the chicken and turn the pieces to coat well. Cover with plastic wrap and marinate in the refrigerator for at least 20 minutes, or preferably overnight.

To grill the chicken, prepare a hot fire in a charcoal grill or preheat a gas grill until very hot. Place the chicken on the grill rack and grill, turning once, for 3 to 4 minutes on each side, until completely cooked through and no longer pink inside. Transfer to a plate and loosely tent with aluminum foil to keep warm.

Bring a large pot of salted water to a boil over high heat. Add the pasta and cook according to the package instructions, until al dente. Drain in a colander, rinse with warm water, and return the pasta to the pot in which it was cooked.

To prepare the sauce, in a large sauté pan over high heat, warm the oil. Add the onion and sauté for 3 to 4 minutes, until soft but not browned. Add the half-and-half and simmer for 5 minutes to cook off the raw taste of the cream. Add the tomatoes and bring back to a simmer. Add the cheese, pepper, and basil and simmer for about 5 minutes, until warmed through. Do not let the sauce boil or it will break (separate). Taste and adjust the seasoning with salt and pepper if necessary. Remove from the heat.

Thinly slice the chicken breasts against the grain. Add the sauce to the pasta and toss well. Add the chicken and toss again. Place the pasta on a large serving platter and garnish with grated cheese and basil. Serve at once.

Asian-Inspired London Broil *(see photo insert)*

SERVES 6 TO 8

Each month our butcher prepares a certain amount of beef for the convent, which enables us to get a wholesale price per pound. It also keeps me on my toes, as I have to come up with new and exciting recipes for the same cuts of meat. You can use this same recipe for London broil, cubed steak for shish kebabs, or, on special occasions, filet mignon.

MARINADE

1 cup vegetable oil
1/4 cup Asian sesame oil
1 cup light soy sauce
1/2 cup firmly packed brown sugar
2 cloves garlic, crushed
2-inch piece fresh ginger, peeled and grated
1/2 cup freshly squeezed lime juice

1 (2-pound) top round London broil
Watercress, arugula, or radicchio, for serving

To prepare the marinade, in a food processor or blender, combine the vegetable oil, sesame oil, soy sauce, brown sugar, garlic, ginger, and lime juice. Process until well incorporated. Reserve half of the marinade in a small bowl for serving.

Place the meat in a large resealable plastic bag. Pour the marinade over the meat. Roll the top of the bag down to expel as much air as possible before sealing. Massage the marinade into the meat to coat evenly. Place in the refrigerator and marinate for at least 1 hour, or preferably overnight. Turn the bag several times to redistribute the marinade.

Prepare a hot fire in a charcoal grill or preheat a gas grill until hot. Remove the meat from the marinade and place on the grill rack. Discard the bag and marinade. Grill the steak, turning once, for 12 to 15 minutes on each side, until it reaches an internal temperature of 160°. The meat should be firm to the touch and slightly pink inside. Remove from the grill and allow to rest for at least 20 minutes before slicing.

Arrange the greens on a large serving platter. Slice the beef against the grain into 1/4-inch-thick slices and arrange on the greens. Serve immediately with the reserved marinade on the side.

Curried Chicken Salad

SERVES 4 TO 6

At my first "real" restaurant job, I learned a version of this chicken salad, which I've updated here to include mango and walnuts. A time-saving tip: buy a rotisserie chicken at your local supermarket. It is delicious, quick, and you don't have to turn your stove on.

1 pound boneless, skinless chicken breasts
1/2 cup chicken stock (page 197)
Salt
Freshly ground black pepper
1/2 cup mayonnaise
2 teaspoons curry powder
1 tablespoon sugar
2 cups diced fresh pineapple, or 1 (16-ounce) can pineapple tidbits, drained
1 cup chopped fresh mango
1/2 cup chopped walnuts
6 slices fresh pineapple, or 1 (16-ounce) can pineapple slices, drained
Chopped fresh parsley, for garnish

Rinse the chicken under cold running water and pat dry with paper towels. In a large sauté pan over high heat, combine the stock and chicken breasts and season with salt and pepper. Cover with a tight-fitting lid and bring to a boil. Decrease the heat to achieve a low simmer and poach the chicken for 15 minutes, until it is cooked through and no longer pink. Transfer the chicken and cooking liquid to a bowl, cover with plastic wrap, and place in the refrigerator until completely cool. Drain and chop into bite-sized pieces.

To assemble the salad, in a large bowl, combine the mayonnaise, curry powder, and sugar. Stir well until thoroughly mixed. Add the chicken, diced pineapple, mango, and walnuts. Toss well to coat. Taste and adjust the seasoning with salt and pepper if necessary.

To serve, place the pineapple slices on a large serving platter. Mound the salad on top and garnish with parsley.

Moderate eating ensures sound slumber
and a clear mind on rising.

—**Sirach 31:20**

Cauliflower with Seasoned Bread Crumbs *(see photo insert)*

SERVES 4 TO 6

Sometimes it's hard to come up with interesting ways to serve the same old vegetables. I have found that serving cauliflower this way brightens up an otherwise dull side dish and makes it palatable to a larger number of the Sisters.

1/4 cup pine nuts
2 tablespoons unsalted butter
1 cup Italian-style seasoned bread crumbs
1/2 cup grated Romano cheese
1 clove garlic, minced
1/2 teaspoon freshly ground black pepper
2 tablespoons chopped fresh parsley
1 head cauliflower, separated into small florets
Salt
2 tablespoons olive oil

Preheat the oven to 350°. Spread the pine nuts on a small baking sheet in a single layer. Place in the oven and toast for 8 to 10 minutes, until golden brown. Remove from the oven and pour onto a plate to cool.

In a small sauté pan over medium-high heat, melt the butter. Transfer to a bowl and toss in the toasted pine nuts, bread crumbs, cheese, garlic, pepper, and parsley.

Bring a large pot of water to a boil over high heat. Alternatively, bring water to a boil in the pan of a steamer with the rack in place. Add the cauliflower to the pot or steamer and cook for 4 to 8 minutes, until fork tender. Drain and place in a serving bowl or on a serving platter.

Season the cauliflower with salt and pepper, drizzle with the oil, and sprinkle with the bread crumb mixture. Serve immediately.

Summertime Pineapple Jell-O Mold

SERVES 6 TO 8

I know gelatin recipes can be clichéd, but this one is really good and the Sisters always enjoy it. Whether you make it in a fancy copper mold or in a regular old bowl, it is sure to please at any barbecue or picnic.

1 cup boiling water
2 (3-ounce) packages lime Jell-O
1 (16-ounce) can crushed pineapple
1 cup ice cubes
1 pint (2 cups) sour cream
1/2 cup chopped walnuts
1/2 cup finely diced celery
Mint sprigs, for garnish

Pour the boiling water into a heatproof bowl, and stir in the Jell-O until completely dissolved. Drain the pineapple, reserving the juice, and add the juice to the ice cubes to make 1 full cup. Add the ice mixture to the gelatin mixture and stir until melted.

Place the sour cream in a separate bowl. Stir with a whisk until smooth. While continuing to whisk, slowly add the gelatin mixture until thoroughly incorporated. Add the pineapple, walnuts, and celery and mix well. Pour into a decorative 6-cup mold or a 2-quart bowl. Cover and place in the refrigerator for at least 3 hours or up to overnight, until firm.

To unmold, fill the sink or a large bowl with hot water. Immerse the mold and twist and shake until the contents separate from the sides. Invert a serving platter over the mold, then, holding the mold and platter firmly, invert them together. Lift off the mold. Garnish with mint sprigs and serve immediately.

Chiffon Cake with Mocha Frosting

SERVES 8 TO 10

This recipe holds a special place in my heart, as a Sister who is no longer with us shared it with me. It had been given to her by an older Sister, and so on and so on, making it a treasured heirloom. The Sisters agree it is just right and brings them back to simpler times. The mocha frosting is as light as a cloud and well worth the preparation time.

2 1/4 cups cake flour
1 1/2 cups granulated sugar
1 tablespoon baking powder
1 teaspoon salt
5 egg yolks
3/4 cup water
1 teaspoon grated lemon zest
1 teaspoon pure vanilla extract
1/2 cup vegetable oil
8 egg whites
1/2 teaspoon cream of tartar
Fresh mint leaves, for garnish

FROSTING
1/2 cup unsalted butter, at room temperature
3 tablespoons unsweetened cocoa powder, plus extra for garnish
3 tablespoons mocha-flavored instant coffee powder
2 cups confectioners' sugar, sifted
1 1/2 teaspoons pure vanilla extract

Preheat the oven to 325°. Have ready an ungreased 9-cup tube or angel food pan.

To make the cake, in a bowl, sift together the cake flour, granulated sugar, baking powder, and salt. Pass the mixture through the sifter again. In a large bowl, combine the egg yolks, water, lemon zest, and vanilla. Using an electric mixer on high speed, beat until pale yellow. Stir in the vegetable oil. In a third bowl, using clean beaters on high speed, beat together the egg whites and cream of tartar, until stiff, moist peaks form. Do not overbeat, as dry egg whites will produce a tough cake.

Gently fold the flour mixture into the yolk mixture. Then fold the egg whites into the flour-egg mixture. Pour the batter into the pan.

Bake for 35 to 45 minutes, until a toothpick inserted into the center comes out clean and dry. Immediately invert the pan onto a cooling rack and allow the cake to cool completely before removing it from the pan.

To prepare the frosting, in a large bowl, combine the butter, cocoa powder, coffee, confectioners' sugar, and vanilla. With an electric mixer on high speed, beat until light and fluffy.

To free the cake from the pan, run a knife around the inside rim. Place the cake on a serving platter and liberally ice with the frosting. Using a sieve, decorate the cake with cocoa powder and garnish with mint leaves. Serve immediately.

Every job has its own perks. Some offer a company car or a gym membership. The Sisters have provided me with a very special perk: the opportunity to bring my children to work with me each day. When I found out that I was pregnant with my son Michael just three months after I was married, the Sisters were quick to assure me that this new addition and any future additions would be welcome at the convent. After much discussion and even more planning, nine-week-old Michael and I were off to work. Once the excitement of our arrival had died down, one Sister was left standing in the kitchen. It was Sister Flavia, or as my kids have come to know her, Sissy.

Sissy asked the prioress if she could devote her days to the care and nurturing of baby Michael, and the prioress agreed. Every day Sister Flavia would pull up in the motorized scooter that she has used since her arthritis made it too difficult to walk, and off she would go, Michael firmly ensconced on her lap. Three years later, her prayers were finally answered and her lap was filled once again with Michael's new baby brother, Matthew. Things proceeded as quietly as they could with two small boys around until I had a particularly strange visit from Sister Florence, who at ninety-four was the oldest Sister in the community. Although her hearing and her sight were failing, her mind was sharp as a tack, and every day she would walk the halls of the convent and stop in the kitchen for a chat.

This particular day, June 6, was a Saturday and Sister Florence was especially happy to see me, as I usually do not work on Saturdays. She pulled me aside, poked my stomach, and asked when I was going to tell her about the new baby. "New baby," I exclaimed, "not yet!" Apparently Florence and Flavia, who were next-door neighbors, had been up to something. On August 6, my husband and I found out we were expecting our third miracle, Hannah Elizabeth. Named after her grandmothers, Hannah is triple blessed, as Flavia agreed to be her godmother.

All three of my children have blossomed in the glow of the Sisters' affection. While my parents joke that the boys will only be attracted to Sicilian widows when they grow up, one thing is for sure—on every day that passes, these Benedictine Sisters make them feel special.

✠ *Sister Flavia with Hannah and Matthew.*

JULY

With the celebration of the Fourth of July, the summer season is in full swing. The Sisters spend this time traveling to visit friends or vacationing at their summer home on the Jersey Shore. Locals like to devote as much time as they can to vacationing "down the shore." Visitors from northern New Jersey spend their days in towns with such quaint names as Avon-by-the-Sea, Point Pleasant Beach, and Seaside Park. Shore-goers from southern New Jersey while away their free time in towns like Avalon, Wildwood, and of course, the infamous Atlantic City.

Nothing in the world compares with spending the day swimming in the ocean and eating sandy sandwiches on a big beach blanket under a brightly colored umbrella. Then, with the salt still sticky on your skin, you walk "the boards" all evening. On the boardwalk, you can climb on to such rides as the Himalaya, the Scrambler, or the ever-popular Giant Ferris Wheel. After that, it's off to play skeeball and video games in the icy-cool air-conditioned arcades.

Classic shore cuisine includes freshly shucked clams, jumbo shrimp cocktails, wedges of pizza, crisp French fries, and the best sausage-and-pepper sandwiches anywhere. Next, throwing caution to the wind, you choose from among a creamy frozen custard, freshly made hot caramel popcorn, or crispy zeppole (fried pizza dough) doused in confectioners' sugar. Just as exhaustion sets in, you join the crowds on the beach and take in the nightly fireworks display, or just sit quietly by the jetty and watch the drawbridges go up and down as fishing boats head out to sea.

The Sisters have a large shore home outside of Atlantic City. It was originally a hotel, so it comes complete with a big kitchen, a spacious dining room, a living room with a fireplace for chilly spring or fall getaway weekends, and at least twelve bedrooms with their own baths. Each Sister schedules her week of vacation and then spends the days enjoying the beach and the boardwalk, reading a good book, or completing a jigsaw puzzle in the large screened-in room. Many Sisters find that just admiring the view from the expansive wrap-around porch is enough activity for the day. They all take turns cooking, so before they go I usually help the assigned cook plan a week's worth of menus. Easy favorites like roast beef and baked ham are good because they can be eaten cold the next day.

Some of the Sisters are no longer able to travel as often as they once did, so I like to incorporate some of the shore themes into my menus at the convent. We have grilled hot dogs with caramelized onions on toasted buns or charbroiled blue cheese burgers served with fresh-cut French fries and creamy coleslaw. Sometimes, for the fun of it, we schedule a "Shore Night" in mid-December and for a brief time return to the lazy, hazy days of July.

The summer produce harvest is now in high gear, and I try to use as much of the abundant and colorful bounty as I can. Everyone knows about Jersey-grown tomatoes and sweet corn, but much more than that is available: squashes, both green and yellow; crisp green beans; fuzzy sweet peaches; plump blueberries; juicy strawberries; fresh herbs. The selection encourages me to be more flexible in my menu planning, so every morning I check what I have on hand, and whatever speaks to me is what is served. Sometimes it is as simple as a platter of sliced tomatoes or a salad of green beans and red onions with an herbed vinaigrette. Other nights it is charbroiled chicken with soy sauce and lemon and grilled corn on the cob slathered in herb butter. Listen to your ingredients and follow where they lead you. Usually they know the way.

Layered Taco Salad with Buttermilk Ranch Dressing

SERVES 6 TO 8

Each month the administration of the convent meets for a council meeting, during which all the subjects important to the Sisters are discussed. The meetings have also grown into informal culinary tastings, as I develop recipes to serve that I wouldn't be able to cook for the whole house. The Sisters on the council liked this salad from its debut and, since then, have requested it often, especially in the summer months.

1 pound ground beef
1 package taco seasoning
1 head iceberg lettuce, cored and thinly sliced
1 pound Cheddar cheese, shredded
2 tomatoes, chopped
2 green bell peppers, stemmed, seeded, and chopped
2 red onions, chopped
1 (15-ounce) can sliced black olives, drained

DRESSING
1 cup mayonnaise
1/2 cup sour cream
1/2 cup buttermilk, or as needed
1 tablespoon chopped fresh parsley
1 teaspoon garlic powder
1 teaspoon onion powder
Salt
Freshly ground black pepper

1 cup prepared spicy salsa
1/2 pint (1 cup) sour cream
1 cup guacamole
Restaurant-style tortilla chips

To prepare the salad, heat a large sauté pan over high heat. Add the ground beef and cook, stirring to break up the lumps, for 15 minutes, until browned. Drain off the excess fat. In a small bowl, combine the taco seasoning with water according to the package instructions. Add the seasoning to the meat, decrease the heat to medium, and simmer for 10 minutes, until the meat is fairly dry. Transfer to a bowl and allow to cool to room temperature.

In a tall-sided glass bowl, layer, in order, the meat, lettuce, cheese, tomatoes, bell peppers, onions, and olives. Cover with plastic wrap and refrigerate for about 1 hour, until chilled.

To prepare the dressing, in a bowl, combine the mayonnaise, sour cream, $1/2$ cup buttermilk, parsley, garlic powder, and onion powder. Whisk together until well mixed and season with salt and pepper. If the dressing seems too thick, add more buttermilk. Taste and adjust the seasoning with salt and pepper if necessary.

To serve, present the salad in the bowl at the table. Offer the dressing, salsa, sour cream, guacamole, and chips on the side.

Blue Cheese Burgers and Hot Dogs with Caramelized Onions

SERVES 6 TO 8

Plain old hamburgers and hot dogs can be too ordinary, so I jazz them up with tangy blue cheese and some slowly cooked onions. To dress them up even more, slather your rolls with butter and garlic and then toast them on the grill while the hot dogs and hamburgers are grilling. This will make a sandwich no guest will soon forget.

HAMBURGERS

1 pound ground beef
2 tablespoons Worcestershire sauce
2 tablespoons chopped fresh parsley
1 teaspoon onion powder
1/2 teaspoon salt
1/2 teaspoon freshly ground black pepper
1/2 pound blue cheese, crumbled

CARAMELIZED ONIONS

2 tablespoons unsalted butter
2 tablespoons corn oil
4 large yellow onions, sliced
1 tablespoon sugar
1 teaspoon salt
1/2 teaspoon freshly ground black pepper

8 hot dogs
8 hot dog buns
4 to 6 hamburger rolls
Steak sauce, ketchup, and assorted mustards, for serving

To prepare the hamburgers, in a large bowl, with your hands, combine the ground beef, Worcestershire sauce, parsley, onion powder, salt, pepper, and blue cheese. Form into 6 small patties or 4 large ones. Place them on a plate, cover with plastic wrap, and refrigerate for 30 minutes to 1 hour.

To prepare the onions, heat a large sauté pan over high heat. Add the butter and oil and swirl until the butter melts. Add the onions and decrease the heat to medium. Sauté for 5 to 8 minutes, until the onions begin to brown and become soft. Add the sugar, salt, and pepper and simmer slowly, without stirring, until the bottom begins to brown. This should take 10 to 15 minutes. Stir slowly, then continue browning and stirring for 5 to 10 minutes, until all the onions are deep brown. If they look dry, add a little liquid such as water, stock, or even beer if that's the nearest liquid to you. Remove from the heat, cover, and keep warm.

To grill the hamburgers and hot dogs, prepare a hot fire in a charcoal grill or preheat a gas grill until very hot. Place the hamburger patties on the grill rack. Score the hot dogs lengthwise and place on the grill rack. If using a charcoal grill, move the burgers and hot dogs away from the hottest area. If using a gas grill, decrease the flame to medium. Grill the meats, turning once. The timing for the burgers will vary according to their size, with the larger ones taking 10 to 12 minutes and the smaller ones 8 to 10 minutes. The burgers are done when they are browned on both sides and reach an internal temperature of 160°. The hot dogs will take about 8 minutes and are done when they are evenly browned and the skin is crispy.

To serve, place the hot dogs on the buns and cover with the caramelized onions. Place the burgers on the hamburger rolls and serve with steak sauce, ketchup, and mustard. The onions also taste great on the burgers!

The Best Barbecued Chicken (page 111) and Backyard Barbecue Potato Salad (page 114)

Quick Quiche (page 75)

Asian-Inspired London Broil (page 94) and Cauliflower with Seasoned Bread Crumbs (page 98)

Peanut Butter Pie with Fudge Topping (page 131)

The Best Barbecued Chicken *(see photo insert)*

SERVES 6 TO 8

This chicken is deceivingly delicious—you can't believe how good it is until you start eating it and can't stop. Be sure to buy at least 50 percent more chicken than you usually need for your family. For some reason, the thighs go particularly fast. If you don't feel like grilling outside, this recipe is equally delicious baked in the oven (bake at 350° for 45 minutes, until the skin is crispy and the meat is cooked through and no longer pink).

4 chicken breast halves, skin on
6 chicken legs, skin on
6 chicken thighs, skin on
1 cup light soy sauce
1/2 cup freshly squeezed lemon juice
2 teaspoons garlic powder
2 tablespoons chopped fresh tarragon, or 2 teaspoons dried tarragon
1 teaspoon paprika
1/2 teaspoon freshly ground black pepper

Rinse the chicken pieces under cold running water and pat dry with paper towels. In a bowl, combine the soy sauce, lemon juice, garlic powder, tarragon, paprika, and pepper. Divide the chicken evenly between 2 large resealable bags. Divide the marinade evenly between the bags. Roll the tops of the bags down to expel as much air as possible before sealing. Massage the marinade into the chicken to coat evenly. Place in the refrigerator and marinate for at least 3 hours, or preferably overnight. Turn the bags several times to redistribute the marinade.

Prepare a hot fire in a charcoal grill or preheat a gas grill until very hot. Place the chicken, skin side down, on the grill rack. Discard the bags and marinade. If using a charcoal grill, move the chicken away from the hottest area. If using a gas grill, decrease the flame to medium-low. Cover the grill. (This will allow the chicken to cook thoroughly without drying out.) Turn the chicken frequently so it cooks evenly and thoroughly. It should be ready in about 35 minutes, or when the internal temperature reaches 165°.

To serve, place the chicken on a large serving platter and let your family and friends go to town.

She procures her food in the summer,
Stores up her provisions in the harvest.

—Proverbs 6:8

Sweet-and-Sour Marinated Carrots

SERVES 4 TO 6

Every now and again, one of the Sisters brings me a family recipe and asks me to try it. This one sounded a bit strange when Sister Joan Loretta brought it to me, but I added a little and subtracted a little and came up with this version. The Sisters love it, and I make it all summer long. The carrots taste best after spending the night in the fridge, and they will keep well for up to a week. In fact, the longer they marinate, the tastier they get.

3 pounds carrots, peeled and sliced on the diagonal (5 cups)
1 (10-ounce) can condensed tomato soup
1 cup sugar
1 tablespoon yellow mustard
1 tablespoon Worcestershire sauce
1/2 cup extra virgin olive oil
3/4 cup red wine vinegar
1 teaspoon salt
1/2 teaspoon freshly ground black pepper
1 green bell pepper, stemmed, seeded, and sliced
1 yellow onion, thinly sliced

Bring a large pot of water to a boil over high heat. Add the carrots and simmer for 5 minutes, until crisp-tender. Drain and rinse under cold water to halt the cooking. Set aside to drain thoroughly.

In a large bowl, combine the soup, sugar, mustard, Worcestershire sauce, oil, vinegar, salt, and black pepper and mix well. Add the carrots, bell pepper, and onion and toss thoroughly. Cover and marinate in the refrigerator for at least 1 hour before serving.

Backyard Barbecue Potato Salad *(see photo insert)*

SERVES 6 TO 8

When a barbecue meal is served, whether it be hot dogs and hamburgers or ribs and chicken, the Sisters always look for my potato salad. Around these parts, your potato salad recipe is as personal as your signature. I add chopped green olives to my salad to set off the creaminess of the mayonnaise and pack an extra punch.

DRESSING
1/2 cup extra virgin olive oil
1/2 cup red wine vinegar
1 tablespoon chopped green bell pepper
1 tablespoon chopped red bell pepper
1 clove garlic, minced
2 tablespoons chopped yellow onion
1 teaspoon salt
1/2 teaspoon freshly ground black pepper

4 pounds russet potatoes, unpeeled
1 1/2 cups mayonnaise
1/4 cup distilled white vinegar
1 yellow onion, chopped
4 celery stalks, chopped
4 hard-boiled eggs, peeled and chopped
1 cup pitted green olives, chopped
3 tablespoons chopped fresh parsley, plus extra for garnish
Paprika, for garnish

To prepare the dressing, combine the oil, vinegar, bell peppers, garlic, onion, salt, and pepper in a small bowl and mix well.

Place the potatoes in a large pot, add cold water to cover, and bring to a boil over high heat. Simmer for 25 to 30 minutes, until fork tender. Drain well. Using a towel or rubber gloves to protect your hands from the heat, peel and quarter the potatoes lengthwise, then cut crosswise into 1-inch pieces. Place in a large bowl and toss with the dressing. Cover with plastic wrap and marinate overnight in the refrigerator, tossing occasionally.

The next day, add the mayonnaise, vinegar, onion, celery, eggs, olives, and parsley and mix thoroughly. Cover and refrigerate until ready to serve.

Transfer the salad to a decorative bowl. Garnish with parsley and paprika and serve.

Green Bean Salad

SERVES 4 TO 6

Some days it seems almost too hot to eat, and on those occasions I prepare a cold buffet. Sliced cold meats and various salads fill out the menu. It never feels complete without this cold bean salad.

1/4 cup pine nuts
1 pound green beans, ends trimmed and halved crosswise
1 pint cherry tomatoes, stemmed
1 red onion, thinly sliced
1/4 cup red wine vinegar
2 tablespoons chopped fresh parsley
2 tablespoons chopped fresh basil
1 teaspoon fresh oregano, or 1/2 teaspoon dried oregano
1/2 teaspoon garlic powder
1/2 cup extra virgin olive oil
Salt
Freshly ground black pepper
2 ounces Romano or Parmesan cheese, shaved

Preheat the oven to 350°. Spread the pine nuts on a small baking sheet in a single layer. Place in the oven and toast for 8 to 10 minutes, until golden brown. Remove from the oven and pour onto a plate to cool.

Bring a pot of salted water to a boil over high heat. Add the green beans and cook for 4 minutes, until crisp-tender. Drain and rinse under cold water to halt the cooking. Place in a large bowl, cover, and refrigerate until chilled.

Cut the cherry tomatoes through the stem ends into halves or quarters, depending on their size. Add to the green beans along with the onion and toss.

To prepare the dressing, in a small bowl, combine the vinegar, parsley, basil, oregano, and garlic powder. Slowly whisk in the olive oil until emulsified and season with salt and pepper. Pour over the beans and toss thoroughly.

To serve, place the salad in a large serving bowl or on a large platter. Sprinkle with the toasted pine nuts and the cheese.

When a just man eats, his hunger is appeased,
but the belly of the wicked always suffers want.

—Proverbs 13:25

Peach and Blueberry Cobbler

SERVES 4 TO 6

Many times during the summer, friends of the Sisters drop off various types of fresh produce. Whether the gifts are from their gardens or from their travels, a brown bag of zucchini or a couple quarts of blueberries are always found treasures. I look forward to these unexpected arrivals and the challenge they present in preparing them the best way.

2 to 3 pounds ripe firm peaches, peeled, pitted, and sliced
1 quart fresh blueberries
2 cups flour
1 teaspoon salt
1 tablespoon baking powder
3 tablespoons chilled unsalted butter
3 tablespoons chilled high-quality vegetable shortening
1 egg
3/4 cup sugar
1 teaspoon ground cinnamon
1/3 cup melted unsalted butter
1 quart high-quality vanilla ice cream (optional)

Preheat the oven to 350°. Grease a 9 by 13-inch baking dish. (A pretty 12-inch quiche dish also makes a nice presentation.)

Place the peaches and berries in the prepared baking dish and toss to mix.

In a large bowl, combine the flour, salt, and baking powder and stir together with a fork. Using a pastry blender or 2 butter knives, cut the butter and shortening into the dry ingredients until the mixture has the consistency of rolled oats. Add the egg, sugar, and cinnamon and mix with a wooden spoon until a crumbly dough forms. Evenly drop the dough by tablespoonfuls onto the fruit. Drizzle the melted butter in and around the pieces of dough.

Bake for 35 minutes, until the crust is golden and the fruit is bubbly. Remove from the oven and let stand for 20 minutes before serving. To serve, place a large spoonful of warm cobbler on a plate along with a scoop of ice cream.

Over the years, the convent has become a popular place to visit, and I have prepared dinner for various guests from many different walks of life, including an archbishop and a few cardinals. On one occasion, I cooked a pot roast dinner with all of the fixings for the Abbot Primate, the head of all Benedictines who is based at the Vatican.

Probably the most interesting guests for whom I have cooked were a group of Tibetan monks who stayed at the convent for a week to observe the Sisters' way of life. Every new aspect of convent life about which they learned filled them with awe and joy. They loved to come into the kitchen and ask about the food and how I prepared it. The monks, through example, taught that the simplest things in life hold the most wonder.

✠ *The library of the mansion.*

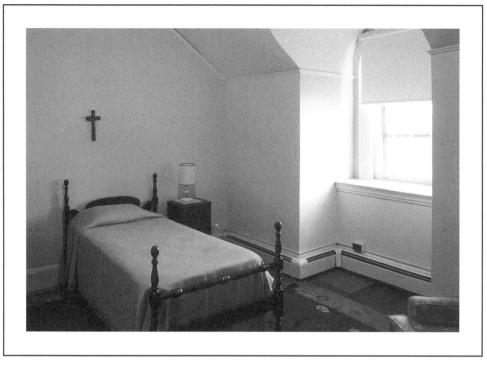

✠ *A typical guest room in the mansion.*

The executives and support staff of Angel Records made up another interesting group. The recording company "discovered" the heavenly voice of Sister Germaine Fritz, a former prioress at the convent, and hired her to sing on an album of chant that was taken from the work of a medieval Benedictine nun named Hildegarde von Bingen. After the successful release and a European tour, Sister Germaine hosted a celebratory dinner at the convent to thank everyone involved.

AUGUST

With the arrival of August, the dog days of summer are upon us. The nights are as warm as the days, and the humidity lingers around 90 percent. The Sisters try to get as much work done as possible early in the day when the heat is not as bad. While the newer buildings in the convent are air-conditioned, the original mansion is quite a heat collector. During my first five years with the Sisters, I cooked in the steamy mansion kitchen.

This time of year I employ a lot of short and sweet dinner ideas. I don't feel like spending hours in the kitchen cooking, and the Sisters don't feel like spending hours in the dining room eating. If the weather is particularly hot and sticky, I make one of my many pasta salads. They are filled with fresh vegetables and cold meats or seafood, and I like to dress them with a light vinaigrette or a lemony dressing. A big plus is that these pasta salads always taste better the next day.

One of my favorite times of the year in the kitchen is late summer. I try to gather and store as many of the fresh fruits and vegetables as I can. I pick blueberries and raspberries and freeze them for holiday cakes and pies. When the nights turn warm, the tomatoes by my kitchen door continue to ripen twenty-four hours a day. When the tomato bushes are bursting with fruit, I take the time to peel and seed the harvest and freeze the resulting concassé for use over the fall and winter. Of course, with canned tomatoes so widely available, I don't need to do this extra work, but I find it spiritually rewarding to preserve the fruits and vegetables that I have nurtured from tiny seedlings. Food always tastes best when the ingredients have been grown in your own garden and lovingly stored away for colder days.

Sliced Beefsteak Tomatoes with Basil and Red Onion

SERVES 4 TO 6

You can also top this salad with fresh mozzarella and roasted peppers or a few anchovy fillets. Served with a crusty baguette, it is perfect for a picnic or a day at the beach.

4 large, ripe beefsteak tomatoes, sliced 1/4 inch thick
1 tablespoon sugar
1 teaspoon garlic powder
Salt
Freshly ground black pepper
1 bunch fresh basil, stemmed and leaves julienned
1 large red onion, thinly sliced
1/2 cup extra virgin olive oil
1/4 cup balsamic vinegar

Arrange the tomato slices on a large serving platter. Sprinkle with the sugar, garlic powder, salt and pepper to taste, and half of the basil.

Arrange the onion slices evenly over the tomatoes. Sprinkle with the remaining basil. Season again with salt and pepper and drizzle the oil and vinegar over the top.

Pesto Fettuccine

SERVES 4 TO 6

The combination of basil, pine nuts, and sharp Romano cheese delivers an absolute flavor explosion. While pesto is most commonly used as a pasta sauce, it is equally good stirred into a hot bowl of vegetable soup or layered with Brie cheese and pastry on a holiday buffet. If you don't have a scale to weigh the basil, use 3 cups of firmly packed leaves and check the flavor and consistency at the end. It should be a thick paste. If the pesto is too thin, add more basil and process again.

PESTO
1/4 pound (about 3 cups) fresh basil leaves
2 teaspoons minced garlic
1/2 cup extra virgin olive oil
1/2 cup pine nuts
3/4 cup grated Romano cheese

1 pound dried fettuccine
Grated Romano cheese, for serving

To make the pesto, rinse the basil leaves, then dry in a lettuce spinner. In a food processor or blender, combine the basil, garlic, oil, pine nuts, and cheese and process until a smooth paste forms. Stop the processor as needed to scrape down the sides of the bowl to achieve a uniform texture. Use immediately, or store in a glass jar with a tight-fitting lid, topped with a thin layer of olive oil, for later use.

Bring a large pot of salted water to a boil over high heat. Add the fettuccine and cook according to the package instructions, until al dente. Drain well.

To serve, divide the pasta among 4 warmed dinner plates or 6 plates for a first course. Spoon a mound of pesto in the center of each serving and sprinkle with cheese. Each guest then tosses his or her own serving.

Thirty-Minute Fresh Tomato Sauce

MAKES 4 CUPS

The embodiment of summer, this sauce has a full, rich taste that is great with pasta but also makes a nice accompaniment to a broiled chicken or grilled fish. The recipe yields enough sauce for 2 pounds of pasta.

4 pounds ripe tomatoes
1/4 cup olive oil
4 cloves garlic, minced
2 yellow onions, chopped
1/2 cup fresh basil leaves, julienned
Salt
Freshly ground black pepper

Bring a large pot of water to a boil over high heat. Prepare a large bowl of ice water, with more ice than water.

With a sharp paring knife, core the tomatoes and then score the bottoms (blossom ends) with an X. Working in batches so as not to crowd the pot, immerse the tomatoes in the boiling water for about 30 seconds, until the skin begins to lift away from the flesh at the X. Remove the tomatoes with a slotted spoon and plunge them into the ice water.

Remove the tomatoes from the ice water and peel away the skins. Cut each tomato in half crosswise and, holding each half cut side down over a bowl, squeeze gently to express all the seeds. Chop the tomatoes into medium pieces. (If desired, these peeled and chopped tomatoes alone can be frozen for future use.)

In a large sauté pan over high heat, warm the olive oil. Add the garlic and onions and sauté for 4 minutes, until soft but not browned. Add the tomatoes and bring to a simmer. Decrease the heat to medium and cook slowly, uncovered, stirring occasionally, for 20 minutes, until the tomatoes are very tender. The tomatoes will produce a lot of liquid. If you like a thicker sauce, continue to cook for about 10 minutes, until the liquid is reduced by half.

Add the basil and simmer for an additional 5 minutes. Season with salt and pepper before serving.

On a man generous with food, blessings are invoked
and this testimony to his goodness is lasting.

—Sirach 31:23

Cold Sesame Noodles with Chicken and Summer Vegetables

SERVES 4 TO 6

These cold noodles only get better with time. Mix the noodles with the marinade and nothing more and you have a great dish. My kids have even asked for them for breakfast. Add the vegetables and chicken when you want to make a delicious and balanced summertime meal.

1 pound boneless, skinless chicken breasts, trimmed of excess fat
Salt
Freshly ground black pepper

DRESSING
1/2 cup light soy sauce
1/4 cup Asian sesame oil
1/4 cup creamy peanut butter
3 tablespoons brown sugar
1 clove garlic, minced
1-inch piece fresh ginger, peeled and grated
2 tablespoons seasoned rice vinegar

1 pound thin rice noodles or angel hair pasta
1 carrot, peeled and thinly sliced
1/2 pound snow peas, ends trimmed
4 green onions, white and tender green parts, sliced
4 plum tomatoes, sliced
1 (16-ounce) can baby corn, drained and rinsed

Preheat the broiler. Season the chicken with salt and pepper and place in a broiling pan. Place under the broiler, turning once, for 10 minutes on each side, until charred. The meat should be firm to the touch and no longer pink. Remove from the broiler and refrigerate until cold, then cut against the grain into thin slices and return to the refrigerator until needed.

To prepare the dressing, in a bowl, combine the soy sauce, sesame oil, peanut butter, sugar, garlic, ginger, and vinegar.

Bring a large pot of salted water to a boil over high heat. Add the noodles and cook according to the package instructions, until al dente. Drain, rinse with warm water, and transfer to a large bowl. Pour the dressing over the noodles, toss to mix, cover, and marinate in the refrigerator for at least 20 minutes or up to overnight. Toss frequently to distribute the dressing evenly.

Bring a small pot of water to a boil over high heat. Add the carrot and snow peas and cook for 4 minutes, until crisp-tender. Drain and rinse under cold water to halt the cooking. Place in a bowl.

To serve, add the chicken, carrot, snow peas, green onions, tomatoes, and corn to the noodles and toss well. Mound a serving on each plate.

Couscous with Feta Cheese and Lemon

SERVES 6 TO 8

Couscous was unknown to the Sisters until I introduced it to them with this salad, which was very well received and has since become a popular favorite on the summer menu. To turn the salad into a delicious, light, and tasty meal, add a pound of cold boiled shrimp.

2 cups chicken stock (page 197)
1 tablespoon plus 1/2 cup extra virgin olive oil
2 cups instant couscous
1/3 cup freshly squeezed lemon juice
2 cloves garlic, minced
3 tablespoons chopped fresh parsley, plus extra for garnish
1/2 teaspoon freshly ground black pepper
Salt
1/2 pound feta cheese, crumbled
1 small red onion, chopped
1 cucumber, peeled, seeded, and chopped
2 plum tomatoes, chopped

In a pot over high heat, combine the chicken stock and the 1 tablespoon olive oil and bring to a boil. Add the couscous, stir well, cover, and remove from the heat. Let stand for 5 minutes, then fluff with a fork.

Transfer the couscous to a large bowl and add the 1/2 cup olive oil, the lemon juice, garlic, parsley, and pepper. Toss to mix, then taste and adjust the seasoning with salt if necessary. Cover loosely and refrigerate for about 1 hour, until chilled.

Remove the couscous from the refrigerator and add the feta cheese, onion, cucumber, and tomatoes and toss well. Taste and adjust the seasoning if necessary. To serve, mound the salad in individual bowls or on a large serving platter and garnish with parsley.

Peanut Butter Pie with Fudge Topping *(see photo insert)*

SERVES 6 TO 8

This recipe has been around the world and back with the various folks that have requested it from me. The first time I made it, the Sisters had never had peanut butter pie, much less one with a layer of fudge and whipped cream garnish. The combination quickly became a favorite. I have since tried many different recipes, and this one is not too rich, not too sweet, and is good both chilled and at room temperature.

CRUST
1¹/₂ cups graham cracker crumbs
¹/₄ cup granulated sugar
¹/₄ cup unsalted butter, at room temperature

FILLING
1 cup heavy cream, chilled
2 tablespoons plus 1 cup confectioners' sugar
1 tablespoon pure vanilla extract
1 (8-ounce) package cream cheese, at room temperature
2 tablespoons unsalted butter, at room temperature
1 cup creamy peanut butter
1 cup (6 ounces) semisweet chocolate chips
Whipped cream, for garnish
Dark chocolate shavings, for garnish

Preheat the oven to 350°. Grease a 9-inch deep-dish pie pan with butter.

To prepare the crust, in a bowl, combine the crumbs, granulated sugar, and butter and mix until the mixture has the consistency of rolled oats. Transfer to the prepared pan and press onto the bottom and all the way up the sides to form a crust. Carefully line with aluminum foil and fill with pie weights or dried beans. Bake for 12 minutes, until golden brown. Remove from the oven and place on a cooling rack for 10 minutes. Carefully remove the pie weights and foil and allow to cool completely on the cooling rack.

To prepare the filling, in a bowl, combine 1/2 cup of the cream with the 2 tablespoons confectioners' sugar and the vanilla. With an electric mixer on high speed, whip until soft peaks form. Set aside.

In a separate bowl, combine the cream cheese, butter, and peanut butter. With the electric mixer on high speed, whip until light and fluffy. Add the 1 cup confectioners' sugar and whip again. Fold in the sweetened whipped cream. Pour the filling into the pie crust. Smooth out to the edges and refrigerate for at least 3 hours.

To prepare the topping, place the chocolate chips in a microwave-proof bowl and microwave on high for 30 seconds; stir vigorously until smooth. Or, place the chocolate chips in the top pan of a double boiler and melt over barely simmering water; stir until smooth. Add the remaining 1/2 cup cream and whisk until thickened. Pour over the top of the pie. Spread to the edges and refrigerate overnight, until set.

To serve, bring the pie to room temperature, if desired, or serve chilled. Cut into wedges and place on dessert plates. Garnish each serving with whipped cream and chocolate shavings.

During the year, I like to make special surprises for the Sisters that they can enjoy at their leisure. At the end of the summer, with fruits and vegetables at their peak of flavor, I make large batches of pesto and fresh tomato sauce that I freeze in Mason jars. Then, when the Sisters go away on vacation or travel to a special friend's house for the holidays, I pull out these vestiges of summer so that they can give them as gifts.

✝ *Me and my famous oatmeal-raisin cookies.*

In the same vein, for Thanksgiving I make large batches of Pumpkin-Walnut Bread and send the loaves off to the residence floors for Thanksgiving morning. Everyone at the convent usually has time only for toast and coffee, as the morning flies by with dinner preparations. This way, the Sisters can have a slice of bread in peace and not have to worry about preparing breakfast. I do the same for Christmas morning with loaves of my Cranberry-Nut Bread.

After the holiday rush, I make large batches of cookie dough and keep them in the freezer for surprise meetings, snowy afternoons, or quick snacks. Oatmeal raisin, chocolate chip, and gingersnap have all been warmly received. Finally, I like to leave a pot of soup bubbling on the stovetop for hours, ensuring a full-bodied, flavorful result. When ready, I serve some of it and freeze the rest in single-serving containers. It is so much better than canned soup, of course, and makes a light nutritious meal for a Sister feeling under the weather.

SEPTEMBER

September is a busy month around the convent. Summer vacation is over and the Sisters have returned to their various positions in the schools. On the grounds of the convent, autumn has begun to tilt her head toward us. The summer plantings of geraniums, impatiens, and pansies flourish in this period of warm days and cool nights, creating beautiful and vibrant flowers. The Sisters take full advantage of them, filling vases with the abundant blooms and using them to decorate the whole convent. I often come into work in the morning and find a freshly picked nosegay on my desk. Elsewhere, the lush green of the trees begins to give way to the reds, oranges, and yellows of fall. Viewed from the windows of the church, the grounds will look like a painting by the end of the month.

Back in the kitchen, I begin to make more complicated stick-to-the-ribs meals. The Sisters' increased workloads and the cooling temperatures combine to reignite appetites. Dishes like Jambalaya and Chili with All the Fixin's remind us that fall is here, and after the hot temperatures of summer we welcome the change. I plan more menus that can be packed for school lunches the next day or heated up for an after-school snack. A lot of these recipes are great one-pot meals—easy to toss together in fifteen minutes and eat in an hour.

September also brings the obligatory school field trips to the local apple orchards, where the Sisters and their students spend the day climbing trees to capture the perfect MacIntosh or Golden Delicious. The trips always yield bushels of apples, gallons of freshly pressed cider, jars of apple butter, and, if everyone is lucky, freshly made cider donuts, still steaming and covered in cinnamon sugar. I use the fruits of their labor in pies, applesauce, and in various apple cakes.

Vegetable and Bean Soup

SERVES 6 TO 8

During the chillier months, I try to keep a pot of homemade soup on the stove during the week to satisfy after-school hunger pangs. A cup of soup and a few crackers are just enough to tide the Sisters over until dinnertime.

3 tablespoons olive oil
2 cloves garlic, minced
1 large yellow onion, chopped
2 carrots, peeled and chopped
4 celery stalks, chopped
1 tablespoon chopped fresh oregano
1 tablespoon chopped fresh basil
2 tablespoons chopped fresh parsley
2 quarts chicken stock (page 197)
1 large potato, peeled and chopped
1 (28-ounce) can diced tomatoes
1 (16-ounce) can kidney beans, drained and rinsed
Salt
Freshly ground black pepper
1/2 cup grated Romano cheese, plus extra for garnish

In a large pot over high heat, warm the olive oil. Add the garlic and sauté for 1 minute, until aromatic. Add the onion, carrots, celery, oregano, basil, and parsley; stir well. Decrease the heat to medium, cover, and allow to sweat for 10 minutes, until soft but not browned. Add the stock, potato, tomatoes, and beans. Increase the heat to high and bring to a boil. Decrease the heat to medium and simmer, uncovered, for 1 hour, until the potatoes are very tender. Season with salt and pepper to taste.

To serve, stir in the cheese and ladle the soup into warmed soup bowls. Garnish with more cheese and serve at once.

Tooty Fruity Sweet-and-Sour Chicken

SERVES 4 TO 6

Want to add an interesting twist to an ordinary evening meal? Serve this dish with white rice and accompany with fortune cookies for dessert.

1 (15-ounce) can pineapple chunks
1/4 cup firmly packed brown sugar
1/4 cup granulated sugar
1/2 cup cider vinegar
2 cups chicken stock (page 197)
5 tablespoons cornstarch
4 tablespoons vegetable oil
1 yellow onion, chopped
1 red bell pepper, stemmed, seeded, and chopped
1 cup snow peas, ends trimmed
2 pounds boneless, skinless chicken breasts, trimmed of excess fat
    and sliced into thin strips
1/4 cup maraschino cherries, halved
Hot cooked white rice, for serving
Soy sauce, for serving
Hot-pepper sauce, for serving

Drain the pineapple in a sieve over a bowl, capturing the juice. Set the pineapple chunks aside. Add the sugars, vinegar, stock, and 4 tablespoons of the cornstarch to the juice, and stir until the cornstarch and sugars dissolve.

In a large nonstick sauté pan over high heat, warm 2 tablespoons of the oil. Add the onion, bell pepper, and snow peas and stir-fry for 2 minutes, until crisp-tender. Transfer to a bowl.

Rinse the chicken breasts under cold running water and pat dry with paper towels. Dust with the remaining 1 tablespoon cornstarch. Reheat the sauté pan over high heat until it is very hot and add the remaining 2 tablespoons oil. When the oil is hot, add the chicken and stir-fry for 8 to 10 minutes, until golden brown and cooked through. Add the reserved pineapple and the vegetables and stir-fry for 1 minute to heat through. Add the juice mixture and bring to a boil. Decrease the heat to medium and simmer for 2 minutes, until thickened. Stir in the cherries.

To serve, spoon a mound of rice onto each warmed dinner plate and ladle the chicken over the top. Offer soy sauce and hot-pepper sauce as condiments.

Chili with All the Fixin's

SERVES 4 TO 6

I'm sure that you have heard of chili recipes that come from a firehouse kitchen. Well, this one comes from a convent kitchen, and it is guaranteed to light a fire in anyone's heart.

2 pounds ground beef or turkey
2 tablespoons vegetable oil
2 large yellow onions, chopped
1 green bell pepper, stemmed, seeded, and chopped
3 celery stalks, chopped
2 (8-ounce) cans tomato sauce
1 (28-ounce) can whole tomatoes, chopped
1 (10-ounce) bottle chili sauce
2 teaspoons ground cumin
2 tablespoons chili powder
1 teaspoon garlic salt
1 (16-ounce) can kidney beans, drained and rinsed
1 pound Cheddar cheese, shredded
1/2 pint (1 cup) sour cream
1 large red onion, chopped
4 cups hot cooked white rice
Restaurant-style tortilla chips

Place a large pot over high heat. When hot, add the ground beef and cook, stirring to break up the lumps, for 15 minutes, until browned. Remove the beef from the pot with a slotted spoon and drain off the excess fat. Place the pot back over high heat and add the oil. When the oil is hot, add the yellow onions, bell pepper, and celery and stir to coat. Cover, decrease the heat to medium, and allow the vegetables to sweat for 10 minutes, until soft but not browned.

(continued)

Return the cooked meat to the pot along with the tomato sauce, tomatoes, chili sauce, cumin, chili powder, and garlic salt. Bring to a boil, stirring frequently. Decrease the heat to low and simmer, uncovered, for 1 hour. Add the beans and simmer for 30 minutes, until the beans are warmed through.

To serve, place the cheese, sour cream, and red onion in small separate bowls to offer as garnishes. Spoon a portion of rice into each warmed soup bowl and ladle the chili over the rice. Set out the garnishes for diners to add to their own servings. Offer the chips on the side for dipping.

One does not eat by bread alone,
but by every word that comes forth
from the mouth of God.

—Matthew 4:4

Jambalaya *(see photo insert)*

SERVES 4 TO 6

This recipe has been my one foray into Cajun cooking. While the flavors are multilayered, they aren't too spicy for the Sisters, and only get better the longer the dish bubbles on the stove. Offer your guests hot-pepper sauce on the side for an added punch.

2 tablespoons vegetable oil
1 1/2 cups chopped deli-style smoked ham
1 yellow onion, chopped
3 celery stalks, chopped
1 green bell pepper, stemmed, seeded, and chopped
1 clove garlic, minced
1 1/2 cups chicken stock (page 197)
2 (8-ounce) cans tomato sauce
1 cup short-grain white rice
1/4 cup chopped fresh parsley, plus extra for garnish
1 bay leaf
1 teaspoon chopped fresh thyme, or 1/2 teaspoon dried thyme
1 teaspoon Worcestershire sauce
Pinch of ground cayenne pepper
2 cups diced cooked chicken
1/2 pound spicy sausage, such as chorizo, chopped

In a large pot over high heat, warm the oil. Add the ham, onion, celery, bell pepper, and garlic and stir to coat. Cover, decrease the heat to medium, and allow the vegetables to sweat for 10 to 15 minutes, until soft but not browned. Add the stock, tomato sauce, rice, parsley, bay leaf, thyme, Worcestershire sauce, cayenne pepper, chicken, and sausage. (Err on the side of caution with the cayenne. You can always add more.) Cover and simmer for about 30 minutes, until the rice is tender. Stir frequently to avoid scorching on the bottom. Remove and discard the bay leaf.

To serve, spoon the stew into warmed wide-rimmed soup bowls and garnish with parsley.

You raise grass for the cattle and vegetation for man's use,

Producing bread from the earth, and wine to gladden man's heart.

—**Psalms 104:14**

Sweet and Savory Corn Bread *(see photo insert)*

SERVES 6 TO 8

The Sisters enjoy this combination of warm corn bread and sweet corn, and it goes well with both the Jambalaya (page 141) and the Chili (page 139). A blend of sweet and savory, this always popular side dish usually ends up on the breakfast table the next day. For a nice presentation for a buffet table, bake the corn bread in a large cast-iron skillet. Just heat it, grease it, pour in the batter, and bake as directed for the baking dish.

2 cups yellow cornmeal
2 cups flour
1/4 cup sugar
2 tablespoons baking powder
1 teaspoon salt
2 cups milk
2 eggs
1/2 cup unsalted butter, melted
1 cup shredded pepper Jack cheese
2 1/2 cups fresh corn kernels (from about 3 ears)
Unsalted butter, for serving

Preheat the oven to 400°. Grease a 9 by 11-inch baking pan with butter.

In a large bowl, combine the cornmeal, flour, sugar, baking powder, and salt. Add the milk, eggs, and melted butter and stir well. Add the cheese and corn and mix well. Pour into the prepared baking pan.

Bake for 25 to 35 minutes, until golden brown and puffy. To serve, cut into squares and serve immediately. Offer butter as an accompaniment.

Mixed Vegetables with Dill

SERVES 6 TO 8

Occasionally I make a vegetable medley to spice things up, so the Sisters don't get bored of having just one vegetable at a time. This medley seems to be especially well received. The addition of the mushrooms makes it a particularly satisfying side dish.

2 pounds baby carrots, peeled
1 (10-ounce) package frozen baby peas
4 tablespoons unsalted butter
1 pound button mushrooms, sliced
2 tablespoons chopped fresh dill
1 teaspoon sugar
Salt
Freshly ground black pepper

Bring a large pot of water to a boil over high heat. Add the carrots and cook for 8 to 10 minutes, until fork tender. Add the peas and stir just until warmed. Drain, place the vegetables in a large bowl, and cover loosely to keep warm.

In a sauté pan over high heat, melt 2 tablespoons of the butter, swirling the pan to avoid burning. Add the mushrooms and sauté, stirring frequently, for 8 to 10 minutes, until dry and tender.

Add the mushrooms to the carrots and peas. Then add the remaining 2 tablespoons butter, the dill, and the sugar, and season with salt and pepper. Toss to mix and serve immediately.

Applesauce Spice Cake

SERVES 6 TO 8

In this part of the country, the accepted symbol for September is the apple, as they are found in abundance in all the local markets. Not only should you shine them up for your favorite teachers, but you can also find all kinds of ways to serve them up. This recipe also makes great cupcakes for a school bake sale.

4 cups flour
2 teaspoons baking powder
1 teaspoon baking soda
1 teaspoon salt
1 teaspoon ground cinnamon
1 teaspoon ground allspice
1 cup unsalted butter or margarine, at room temperature
1 1/2 cups firmly packed light brown sugar
1/2 cup milk
1 1/2 cups applesauce
4 eggs
1 cup golden raisins

FROSTING
1 1/2 cups unsalted butter, at room temperature
1 1/2 cups high-quality vegetable shortening, at room temperature
1 pound confectioners' sugar, sifted
1 teaspoon ground cinnamon
1 teaspoon ground allspice
1/4 teaspoon ground nutmeg

Cinnamon sugar, for garnish

Preheat the oven to 350°. Butter and flour 3 round cake pans, each 9 inches in diameter.

To prepare the cake, in a bowl, stir together the flour, baking powder, baking soda, salt, cinnamon, and allspice. In another large bowl, combine the butter and brown sugar. With an electric mixer on high speed, beat together until light and fluffy. Add the milk and applesauce and beat well. Add the eggs one at a time, mixing well after each addition.

Add the flour mixture to the butter mixture in thirds, scraping down the sides of the bowl after each addition. Stir in the raisins. Divide the batter evenly among the 3 prepared pans.

Place in the oven and bake for 25 to 30 minutes, until a toothpick inserted into the center comes out dry. Allow to cool for 10 minutes in the pans on cooling racks and then invert onto the racks to cool completely.

To prepare the frosting, in a large bowl, combine the butter, shortening, confectioners' sugar, cinnamon, allspice, and nutmeg. With an electric mixer on high speed, beat for 3 to 6 minutes, until light and fluffy.

To assemble the cake, place 1 cake layer on an attractive serving plate. Spread one-quarter of the frosting over the top. Top with another layer and repeat with another one-quarter of the frosting. Top with the third layer and use the remaining frosting to frost the top and sides of the cake. Garnish with cinnamon sugar and serve.

The rhythm of the Sisters gathering for prayer has become part of my own personal clock. It is not uncommon for one of the Sisters to pop her head into the kitchen to ask if the bell has rung for prayers, and somehow I always know whether it has or not. The Sisters often tell me I am an honorary member of the order. In fact, my son Michael bestowed my nickname, Sister Mommy, on me when he was about two, as everyone else he knew had that title.

The Sisters pray together five times each day. On weekdays, they first celebrate Morning Praise at 6:05 A.M. and then Mass at 6:30 A.M. (their mornings start a bit later on the weekends). At midday, they gather again for Noonday Prayer to pray and meditate. At 5:00 P.M., they assemble to say Vespers before dinner, and then lastly they come together at 6:45 P.M. to say Compline or Night Prayer, which ends the day and sends them off to bed prepared for the next day and its challenges.

✛ *The Sisters at prayer.*

OCTOBER

Finally, fall is officially here. The crisp days of autumn are filled with the crunch of fallen leaves underfoot and the smell of warm spiced apple cider wafting in the air. My sons, Michael and Matthew, are busy all day at school, but Sister Flavia and my daughter, Hannah, take full advantage of the warm afternoons by strolling around the grounds and picking up only the most beautiful leaves to show Mommy.

The calendar is brimming this month with Columbus Day, Halloween, and a large number of the Sisters' feast days. Some months more than others are filled with feast days, but there is no rhyme or reason to their frequency or why the month of October, with about a dozen feast-day celebrations, is so popular. Since the Sisters choose their feast-day menus, I act as a kind of culinary cop. I make sure we don't have three nights in a row with the same entrée or seven nights of mashed rutabagas, as much as they *love* their mashed rutabagas.

On the other days, I try to fill the menus with taste treats that have not been around for several months. Pumpkin breads, spicy gingersnaps, and other fall favorites pop up frequently, as sweaters and jackets come out of their summer storage. Many of the Sisters are of German descent, so they enjoy the addition of such menu items as Sausage, Peppers, Onions, and Potatoes and Creamed Brussels Sprouts with Bacon and Onions. Along another line of inspiration, two Sisters are originally from Vietnam and have taught me many

Asian-inspired dishes. Wraps of lettuce, mint, and cold meats with different dipping sauces have become commonplace around here, and I also have a newfound appreciation for tofu. While many of the Sisters think these are great lunch ideas, they are still somewhat resistant to giving up their familiar meat-and-potatoes dinner meal. Therefore, the Mahogany Chicken, which is a bit more traditional, albeit with some of my contemporary touches, has been a big hit in the evening.

Columbus Day and Halloween are the big national holidays in the October schedule. Because Christopher Columbus was Italian, the holiday is festively celebrated both at the convent and in the surrounding Italian communities. I make a meal that draws heavily on my Italian roots. Fresh from scratch Caesar salad is usually followed by a big spaghetti dinner complete with meatballs, sausage, and my grandmother's bracciole bubbling in the sauce. Homemade tiramisu and anisette cookies finish off the feast with a special touch. Just when the memory of this meal begins to fade, Halloween rolls around with its costume parties and school parades. I try to use a light hand when I plan the All Hallows' Eve dinner, as everyone has spent the day sampling candy and cupcakes. To end the day, I send a platter of fragrant Pumpkin-Walnut Bread to each floor in the residence for the Sisters to enjoy quietly with a cup of tea.

Greek Salad

SERVES 4 TO 6

This salad has all you could want: crisp romaine lettuce, a variety of vegetables and garnishes, and feta cheese, the latter adding a wonderful tangy taste and creamy texture.

2 heads romaine lettuce
1 cucumber, peeled and chopped
3 celery stalks, chopped
1 large tomato, chopped
1 (15-ounce) can pitted small black olives, drained

DRESSING
1/2 cup extra virgin olive oil
1/4 cup red wine vinegar
1 teaspoon onion salt
1/2 teaspoon freshly ground black pepper
1/2 teaspoon dried oregano
Salt

1/2 pound feta cheese, crumbled

Chop the lettuce into bite-sized pieces, rinse thoroughly in a large amount of water, and drain. Dry in a lettuce spinner. In a large salad bowl, combine the lettuce, cucumber, celery, tomato, and olives. Toss well. Cover with a damp paper towel and refrigerate until ready to serve.

To prepare the dressing, in a bowl, combine the oil, vinegar, onion salt, pepper, and oregano. Mix well with a wire whisk. Taste and adjust the seasoning with salt and pepper if necessary.

Add the feta cheese and dressing to the bowl and toss well. Serve immediately.

Sausage, Peppers, Onions, and Potatoes

SERVES 4 TO 6

My mother originated this dish, and I have never forgotten the aroma of the vinegar-scented potatoes and savory sausages slowly cooking together in our family kitchen. To help the Sisters keep their cholesterol down, I occasionally make this recipe with chicken or turkey sausage rather than the more traditional pork. I find that the end product is equally delicious.

2 tablespoons olive oil
2 pounds sweet Italian sausages, cut into 2-inch pieces
4 large yellow onions, sliced
2 large green bell peppers, stemmed, seeded, and sliced
2 large red bell peppers, stemmed, seeded, and sliced
4 large russet potatoes, peeled and cubed
1 tablespoon salt
1 teaspoon freshly ground black pepper
1/2 cup distilled white vinegar
1/2 cup chicken stock (page 197)

In a large sauté pan over high heat, warm the oil. Add the sausages and cook, piercing with a fork to prevent shrinking and turning as necessary to cook evenly, for 8 to 10 minutes, until browned on all sides. Transfer to a plate and keep warm.

Add the onions, bell peppers, potatoes, salt, and pepper to the same pan and stir well. Decrease the heat to medium, cover, and allow the vegetables to cook slowly, stirring occasionally, for 10 to 15 minutes, until crisp-tender. Add the vinegar and stock and deglaze the pan, scraping up any brown bits with a wooden spatula. Return the sausages to the pan and stir gently. Decrease the heat to low, cover, and simmer slowly for 20 minutes, until the potatoes are soft and creamy. Taste and adjust the seasoning with salt, pepper, and vinegar if necessary.

To serve, place a bed of the vegetables on warmed dinner plates and top each serving with an equal amount of the sausage pieces. Serve at once.

Rid your heart of all deceit. Never give a hollow greeting of peace or turn away when someone needs your love.

—The Rule of Saint Benedict, chapter 4

Mahogany Chicken

SERVES 4 TO 6

The amount of ginger and garlic in this recipe seems excessive, but the results are excellent. As several of the Vietnamese Sisters have explained to me, garlic and ginger can act as detoxifiers for the chicken, drawing out impurities such as bad flavors, chemicals, and spirits. The dish is wonderful accompanied with rice and a steamed vegetable.

6 chicken legs
6 chicken thighs
1/4 cup peanut oil
1/2 cup chopped garlic
1/2 cup peeled and chopped fresh ginger
1/2 cup low-sodium soy sauce
2 tablespoons sugar
3 to 4 tablespoons water

Rinse the chicken under cold running water and pat dry with paper towels. With a sharp knife, score the skin around the base of the legs and peel the skin off. Peel the skin off the thighs as well.

Heat a wok or heavy-bottomed sauté pan over high heat. Add the oil. When the oil is hot, add the garlic and ginger and stir-fry for about 1 minute, until aromatic. Add the chicken and stir-fry for 8 to 10 minutes, until browned on all sides. Decrease the heat to medium, cover, and cook for 20 minutes, until cooked through. Remove the pan from the heat and drain off all of the liquid, garlic, and ginger. It is very important that the pan be as dry as possible.

Return the pan to high heat. When it is hot, add the soy sauce and sprinkle the meat with the sugar. As the soy sauce reduces, constantly turn the chicken until it is glazed a deep mahogany brown. Add the water as needed if the soy reduces too quickly. This step should take about 5 minutes.

Transfer the chicken to a serving dish. Serve each guest their choice of drumsticks or thighs.

Scallops with Turmeric-Scented Cream Sauce

SERVES 4 *(see photo insert)*

Big, succulent sea scallops are a personal favorite of mine, as there is so much flavor and texture packed into such small packages. This recipe is a bit on the fussy side, but it is well worth it. Whenever I serve it, the Sisters always comment that they feel like they have been out to dinner at a fancy restaurant.

2 pounds sea scallops
1/2 cup flour
1 tablespoon chili powder
1 teaspoon salt
Vegetable oil, for sautéing
1 red bell pepper, stemmed, seeded, and chopped
1 small yellow onion, chopped
1 teaspoon ground turmeric
1/2 cup dry white wine
1 cup heavy cream
1/2 teaspoon salt
1/4 teaspoon freshly ground black pepper

Rinse the scallops under cold running water and pat dry with paper towels. On a large piece of waxed paper, combine the flour, chili powder, and salt.

Place a large sauté pan over high heat and add enough oil to coat the bottom lightly and evenly. Dredge the scallops in the flour mixture, shake off the excess, and place in the hot pan. Cook, turning once, for 1 to 2 minutes, until browned on both sides. Transfer to a plate and cover loosely to keep warm.

Add 1 tablespoon oil to the same sauté pan over high heat. When the oil is hot, add the bell pepper, onion, and turmeric and sauté for 2 minutes, until crisp.

Add the wine and deglaze the pan, scraping up any brown bits with a wooden spatula. When the wine has reduced by one-half, after about 8 minutes, add the cream, salt, and pepper. Decrease the heat to medium-high and simmer for 10 minutes, until the sauce has reduced by one-third.

To serve, place 4 to 6 scallops on each warmed dinner plate and drizzle the sauce over the top. Serve immediately.

As with the riches of a banquet shall my soul be satisfied.

—Psalms 63:6

Green Beans Amandine with Brown Butter

SERVES 4 TO 6

Browning the butter a bit lifts this dish out of the ordinary. The butter heightens the flavor of the almonds while perfectly complementing the crisp beans.

1 pound green beans, ends trimmed
2 tablespoons unsalted butter
1/2 cup sliced almonds, plus extra for garnish
1 teaspoon sugar
Salt
Freshly ground black pepper

Bring a large pot of water to a boil over high heat. Add the green beans and cook for 3 to 4 minutes, until crisp-tender and bright green. Drain, place in a bowl, and keep warm.

In a small sauté pan over medium heat, melt the butter. As it pools, constantly swirl it in the pan. When it begins to brown at the edges, remove the pan from the heat and add the almonds. Swirl to coat the almonds with the butter and then pour over the green beans. Add the sugar, salt, and pepper and toss well. Serve immediately, garnished with almonds.

Roasted Turkey with an Herbed Rub and Pan Gravy (page 171), Walnut and Mushroom Stuffing (page 173), and Homemade Cranberry Sauce (page 174)

Scallops with Turmeric-Scented Cream Sauce (page 156)

Jambalaya (page 141) and Sweet and Savory Corn Bread (page 143)

Cranberry-Nut Bread (page 192) and Pignoli Cookies (page 194)

Creamed Brussels Sprouts with Bacon and Onions

SERVES 4 TO 6

The difference between fresh and frozen Brussels sprouts can make a convert out of the biggest sprout hater in the world. But if frozen is all you have, don't overcook them and they should be fine. If you are still disappointed, this sauce is delicious used with other winter vegetables such as lima beans or spinach.

2 pounds Brussels sprouts, trimmed
1/2 pound bacon, chopped
1 large yellow onion, chopped
2 tablespoons flour
1 cup half-and-half
Salt
Freshly ground black pepper
Crisp crumbled bacon, for garnish

Place a large pot of salted water over high heat and bring to a boil. Add the sprouts and cook for 4 to 5 minutes, until fork tender. Drain, place in a bowl, and keep warm.

In a large sauté pan over high heat, cook the bacon for 5 minutes, until it renders its fat and begins to brown. Add the onion, decrease the heat to medium, and sauté for 3 minutes, until the onion is soft but not browned. Drain off all but about 2 tablespoons of the bacon fat. Sprinkle in the flour and stir until the onion mixture is well coated. Add the half-and-half, and bring the mixture to a gentle boil. Cook for about 5 minutes to cook off the raw taste of the flour and cream.

Return the sprouts to the pan and stir to coat with the sauce. Reheat the sprouts to serving temperature and season with salt and pepper to taste. To serve, transfer the sprouts and sauce to a warmed serving bowl and garnish with crumbled bacon. Serve immediately.

Pumpkin-Walnut Bread

MAKES 2 LARGE LOAVES OR I BUNDT CAKE

Yearly pumpkin picking is enjoyed by nearly every schoolchild in the area. My husband and I pack up the kids on a sunny Saturday and travel out to the farms in northern and western New Jersey to select the best carving pumpkins available. Served with soft butter or cream cheese and lots of cold milk or warm cider, this bread is a welcome homecoming after a chilly day in the pumpkin patch.

3$1/2$ cups flour
2 teaspoons baking soda
2 teaspoons ground cinnamon
$1/2$ teaspoon ground nutmeg
1$1/2$ teaspoons salt
3 cups sugar
1 cup vegetable oil
4 eggs
$2/3$ cup water
2 cups canned pumpkin purée
1 cup chopped walnuts

Preheat the oven to 350°. Butter and flour 2 loaf pans or a 6-cup Bundt pan.

Into a bowl, sift together the flour, baking soda, cinnamon, nutmeg, and salt. In a separate large bowl, combine the sugar, oil, and eggs. With an electric mixer on high speed, beat until pale yellow and fluffy. Add the water and pumpkin purée and stir until thoroughly incorporated. Slowly fold in the dry ingredients and then the walnuts. Pour the batter into the prepared pan(s).

Bake for 35 to 45 minutes for the loaf pans or 55 to 60 minutes for the Bundt pan, until a toothpick inserted into the center comes out clean. Remove from the oven and allow to rest for 10 minutes in the pan(s) on a cooling rack, then invert onto the rack and allow to cool completely before slicing . . . if you can.

The Sisters gather every day for dinner at 5:30 P.M. sharp! The dining and kitchen area is comprised of several components. The bright and airy dining room is decorated in shades of rose and robin's egg blue. One side is completely lined with large windows that are artfully dressed by the house's resident upholsterer and seamstress, Sister Ruth. The room can sit up to a hundred comfortably, and often does for large feast days.

Across the hall is the service area with a large steam table and racks for plates, silverware, glasses, and the like. Each night, three Sisters assist in the service of dinner. Two work in the dish room washing the dishes and serving utensils, and one does table waiting, which entails removing the covers on the food, exchanging the salad for the dessert, and bringing the empty pans back into the kitchen for cleanup.

Each meal is served family style. After grace, the diners seated at table number one walk over to the service area and help themselves. Then those from table number two serve themselves, and so on. The numbers rotate, so that no one table is always the first or the last to eat. If you are at table number eight for the night, you can usually eat as much as you want, as it's the last table to go. After dessert and coffee, each Sister brings her own plates to the dish area, where a small but handy restaurant-style dishwasher waits to do most of the after-dinner dirty work.

✠ *The dining room.*

NOVEMBER

As November opens, a final layer of fallen leaves covers the ground. The days are short and the evenings long. The weather is still comfortable though—warm enough for a late afternoon walk as the sun sets. The Sisters are busy with their work and are looking forward to the upcoming Thanksgiving holiday and to the Christmas season right around the corner.

Daily life in the November kitchen is quite hectic, with menus that revolve around many fall classics, especially the traditionally prepared German Sauerbraten with Quick Dumplings and Ginger Gravy that all the Sisters enjoy. I only prepare this time-consuming dish twice during the year, which makes the Sisters especially appreciative. Other menu choices tend to be light, as there are so many opportunities to overindulge at this time of year. Sesame-Marinated Salmon Fillets are a good example of this, and any leftovers are delicious served cold the next day for lunch.

Thanksgiving is eagerly awaited by all of the Sisters. The day is devoted to family and friends, both near and far. In years past, the Thanksgiving dinner was prepared by one of the Sisters' families. The cooks would troop in early Thanksgiving morning, sometimes showing up before six o'clock. They would prepare the turkeys and stuffing, mashed potatoes and candied yams, turnips and gravy, cranberry sauce and relish, and, last but not least, homemade pies in several flavors. Then, after an eleven o'clock Mass of Thanksgiving, the community and all the family and friends in attendance would sit down to a feast fit for royalty, prepared with great love and respect.

As the years have passed, and the community has changed with the comings and goings of the Sisters, the second cook (who normally only works on weekends) and I do all of the Thanksgiving preparations. On Wednesday, I stuff and roast four twenty-five pound turkeys with my famous mushroom and walnut stuffing. I cook the turkeys until they are nearly done, then on Thanksgiving Day, the second cook comes in to finish them; make the salads, sauces, and desserts; and serve the Sisters their meal.

In a perfect world, on Thanksgiving I would be at the convent and at home with my family, but preparing the meal this way in a sense allows me to be in both places at the same time. One of the things that drew me to this job was that it permitted me to spend holidays with my family. While I was working in restaurants, I never got holidays or weekends off. Thanksgiving, especially, is a time that I step back and enjoy the fruits of my labor and appreciate the friends and family gathered around my table.

Antipasto Salad

SERVES 6 TO 8

Many Italian families, including my own, serve both an antipasto course and a pasta course at their holiday tables. When I was growing up, my grandmother prepared so much food that eating Thanksgiving dinner took about four hours. We had all of the Italian favorites, such as lasagna and this antipasto, as well as the American standards like turkey and homemade cranberry sauce.

10 slices deli-style smoked ham
10 slices dry salami
1 head romaine lettuce, cored and thinly sliced crosswise
1 cup sliced roasted red bell peppers (page 201)
1 (16-ounce) can artichoke hearts, drained and quartered
1 (10-ounce) jar pimiento-stuffed green olives, drained
1 (15-ounce) can pitted small black olives, drained
1 pound fresh mozzarella cheese, sliced
1/2 pound sharp provolone cheese, cut into 1/2-inch cubes
4 hard-boiled eggs, peeled and halved lengthwise
8 anchovy fillets

DRESSING
1/2 cup olive oil
1/4 cup red wine vinegar
1 teaspoon onion salt
1 tablespoon chopped fresh oregano
1 tablespoon chopped fresh basil
2 tablespoons chopped fresh parsley

To prepare the salad, alternate slices of the ham and salami around the rim of a large serving platter; do not allow them to overhang the edge. Cover the remainder of the platter with a bed of lettuce. Place the red peppers in the center of the lettuce. Arrange the artichoke hearts around the peppers. Arrange the olives, cheeses, and eggs around the artichokes. Arrange the anchovy fillets on top of the eggs. Cover loosely and refrigerate until ready to serve.

To prepare the dressing, in a small bowl, combine the oil, vinegar, onion salt, oregano, basil, and parsley. To serve, drizzle the dressing over the platter.

Bind yourself to no oath lest it prove to be false,
but speak the truth with heart and tongue.

—The Rule of Saint Benedict, chapter 4

Sesame-Marinated Salmon Fillets

SERVES 4

I generally use the grill for this recipe, as I like to barbecue all year long, no matter the weather, but the salmon is equally tasty when baked. Sliced oranges and melon make nice garnishes.

4 (6-ounce) salmon fillets
1/2 cup light soy sauce
1/4 cup Asian sesame oil
1 teaspoon minced garlic
1 teaspoon peeled and grated fresh ginger

Rinse the salmon under cold running water and pat dry with paper towels. Run your fingertips along the flesh to make sure all of the bones have been removed.

In a shallow baking dish, combine the soy sauce, sesame oil, garlic, and ginger. Place the salmon in the marinade and turn to coat. Cover and refrigerate for 30 minutes, turning every 10 minutes.

Preheat the oven to 350°. Remove the salmon from the marinade and place in another baking dish. Bake, turning once, for 5 minutes on each side, until the flesh flakes when pressed gently with a fork. Do not overcook. Transfer to a warmed serving dish and serve immediately.

Sauerbraten with Quick Dumplings and Ginger Gravy

SERVES 4 TO 6

Sister Andrea's feast day falls in November and every year I make from-scratch, honest-to-goodness real sauerbraten to celebrate it. The traditional method is disappearing, and the end product is fully worth all of the time and effort. When I was first asked to prepare sauerbraten, I was a little nervous, as I had never made or even eaten it before. I spent several days researching the preparation and compiling what I thought were the high points from several recipes. I went back to recipes from the early 1900s, hoping to capture what the early German American cooks were trying to impart. While I thought my first offering was terrible, the Sisters were very receptive and said that it was just like their mothers had made. With each subsequent attempt, they say it gets better and better. This recipe is based on my most recent preparation and, I think, my best.

1 large yellow onion, sliced
16 black peppercorns
16 whole cloves
3 bay leaves
1 (2- to 3-pound) beef rump or pot roast
1 quart water
1 quart distilled white vinegar
1/2 cup flour
Salt
Freshly ground black pepper
1/4 cup vegetable oil

DUMPLINGS
4 cups flour
2 teaspoons salt
2 tablespoons baking powder
6 tablespoons chilled butter
6 tablespoons chilled high-quality vegetable shortening

2 tablespoons chopped fresh parsley

1/2 teaspoon freshly ground black pepper

3/4 cup water

GRAVY

2 cups beef stock (page 199)

1 cup sugar

2 tablespoons ground ginger

1/2 cup flour

1 cup water

Salt

Freshly ground black pepper

To marinate the meat, 4 days in advance of cooking, select a deep, nonreactive container large enough to hold the meat completely covered by the marinade. Place half of the onion, peppercorns, cloves, and bay leaves in the bottom of the container. Place the roast on top and cover with the remaining onion, peppercorns, cloves, and bay leaves. Pour in the water and vinegar. Cover tightly and place in the refrigerator for 4 days, turning occasionally with a fork or tongs.

Preheat the oven to 350°. Remove the meat from the marinade and pat dry with paper towels. Transfer the onion to a large roasting pan, reserving the marinade liquid. On a piece of waxed paper, combine the flour, salt, and pepper. Dredge the roast in the flour mixture.

Heat a large sauté pan over high heat and add the oil. When the oil is hot, place the roast in the pan and sear on all sides for 4 to 5 minutes, until browned. Transfer to the roasting pan on top of the onion. Pour in the reserved marinade to a depth of 1 inch or so. Cover tightly and roast for 2 to 2 1/2 hours, until fork tender. Remove from the oven and let stand for 20 minutes.

(continued)

To prepare the dumplings, in a large bowl, combine the flour, salt, and baking powder and stir together with a fork. Using a pastry blender or 2 butter knives, cut the butter and shortening into the dry ingredients until the mixture has the consistency of rolled oats. Add the parsley, pepper, and water and mix thoroughly with a wooden spoon until a soft dough forms. Add more water if the dough seems too dry.

Place a large pot of salted water over high heat and bring to a boil. Decrease the heat to medium to achieve a simmer. With a large spoon or small ice-cream scoop, drop spoonfuls of the batter into the water. You should have 18 dumplings. Cover and cook at a simmer for 8 to 10 minutes, until the dumplings are light and fluffy and cooked through. They will float when done. Do not allow the water to return to a boil. With a slotted spoon, transfer the dumplings to a serving platter, cover loosely, and keep warm.

Remove the roast from the roasting pan, place on the serving platter, and keep warm. Strain the pan juices, reserving 2 cups and discarding the remainder. To prepare the gravy, place the reserved pan juices, beef stock, sugar, and ginger in a saucepan over high heat and bring to a boil. In a bowl, combine the flour and water and whisk until smooth. Add to the gravy and whisk continuously until well incorporated. Bring back to a boil and decrease the heat to medium. Simmer for 20 minutes, until glossy and thickened. Taste and adjust the seasoning with a little more ginger if necessary. If it is too tart, add a little more sugar. Finally, season with salt and pepper.

To serve, slice the roast into 1/4-inch-thick slices. Serve each guest 2 slices of roast and 2 dumplings, both drizzled with the gravy. Serve any additional dumplings and gravy on the side.

Roasted Turkey with an Herbed Rub and Pan Gravy

SERVES 6 TO 8 *(see photo insert)*

Whenever I roast poultry, I rub lots of olive oil and herbs into the skin to make the meat moist and the skin crispy. The seasonings also give the bird a deep golden color and succulent flavor. For a special Thanksgiving presentation, I garnish the turkey platter with fresh parsley or kale and small apples or baby pears. The fruit is anchored with bamboo skewers tucked under the turkey.

1 (14- to 20-pound) turkey
6 cups Walnut and Mushroom Stuffing (page 173)
1 cup olive oil
1 tablespoon salt
2 teaspoons freshly ground black pepper
1 tablespoon chopped fresh thyme, or 1 teaspoon dried thyme
1 tablespoon chopped fresh sage, or 1 teaspoon dried sage
1 teaspoon dried marjoram leaves
1 tablespoon garlic powder
1 tablespoon paprika
1 yellow onion, sliced
2 carrots, peeled and quartered crosswise
2 celery stalks, cut crosswise into thirds
1/2 cup flour
1 cup water

If the turkey was frozen and is not completely thawed, place it in a basin of cool water in the sink. Run the faucet slowly to allow the water in the basin to change continuously.

Preheat the oven to 325°. Remove the giblets and neck from the cavity of the turkey and reserve. Rinse the turkey both inside and out under cold running water and pat dry with paper towels. Stuff the neck cavity and the body cavity with the stuffing.

(continued)

In a bowl, combine the oil, salt, pepper, thyme, sage, marjoram, garlic powder, and paprika. Mix well to form a paste. In the bottom of a large roasting pan, place the onion, carrots, and celery. Distribute the giblets and neck around the pan. Place the turkey in the pan, tucking the wings under the bird. Rub the oil-herb mixture all over the turkey, getting into all the nooks and crannies. Drizzle any extra over the top of the turkey before it goes into the oven.

Tuck a piece of aluminum foil around the opening between the legs to protect the stuffing from burning. Tie the legs together high up on the breast with kitchen string or a long piece of crumpled foil. Cover the whole roasting pan tightly with foil to seal in the juices. Place in the oven and roast, planning 15 minutes per pound, for 3 1/2 to 5 hours, until it reaches an internal temperature of 165°. The thermometer should be inserted at the thigh joint. In the last hour of cooking, remove the foil to allow the skin to brown.

Remove the pan from the oven very carefully, as quite a bit of juice will have accumulated. Cover the pan loosely and allow to rest for at least 20 minutes. Transfer the turkey to a large serving platter and cover loosely again. Transfer the pan juices and vegetables to a saucepan to make the gravy. Allow to sit for a few minutes until the fat rises to the surface, then skim off as much fat as possible.

In a small bowl, combine the flour and water. Place the pan of juices over high heat and bring to a boil. Decrease the heat to medium and slowly stir in the flour mixture. Simmer for a few minutes to cook off the raw flavor of the flour. Taste and season with salt and pepper. Strain through a fine-mesh sieve and transfer to a warmed gravy boat.

To serve, scoop the stuffing out of the turkey into a serving bowl. Carve the turkey at the table, offering each guest their choice of light or dark meat. Place a serving of stuffing next to the turkey on each plate and spoon a ladle of the gravy over the top.

Walnut and Mushroom Stuffing *(see photo insert)*

MAKES 6 CUPS

This is the Sisters' favorite stuffing recipe. It is a great accompaniment to the Thanksgiving turkey, as it doesn't provide competition. For food safety reasons, the stuffing should be made a day in advance so that it can be chilled before it is placed in the bird. Once the turkey is stuffed, roast it immediately.

2 tablespoons plus 1/2 cup unsalted butter
1 yellow onion, chopped
1 pound button mushrooms, sliced
2 (16-ounce) loaves day-old sourdough bread, cut into 1/4-inch cubes
1 tablespoon fresh thyme leaves
1 tablespoon chopped fresh sage
1 teaspoon dried marjoram
1 teaspoon salt
1/2 teaspoon freshly ground black pepper
1 cup chopped walnuts
2 cups boiling water

In a small sauté pan over medium heat, melt the 2 tablespoons butter. Add the onion and sauté for about 5 minutes, until soft. Add the mushrooms and sauté for 5 minutes, until soft. Transfer to a large bowl. Add the bread, thyme, sage, marjoram, salt, and pepper and toss well. Add the walnuts and toss well.

Place the 1/2 cup butter in a heatproof bowl and pour the boiling water over it. Stir constantly until the butter melts, then pour over the bread mixture. Stir well and cover tightly with plastic wrap. Set aside until cooled, then uncover and fluff with a fork. Cover and refrigerate until completely cooled, preferably overnight.

Homemade Cranberry Sauce *(see photo insert)*

SERVES 4 TO 6

You know that feeling that you get right before you board a giant roller coaster? That is how I feel before I make my cranberry sauce. It is always a challenge and I am always afraid it won't gel correctly, but somehow it always does. This recipe is so good that you will never buy another can of cranberry sauce. For best results, prepare the sauce the day before serving it.

1 (12-ounce) bag fresh cranberries (3 cups)
1 cup water
2 to 3 cups sugar
1 tablespoon grated orange zest

Rinse the berries and discard any soft or wrinkled ones. Place in a nonreactive saucepan over high heat and add the water. Bring to a boil and you will begin to hear the berries pop. Once they start popping, boil for 5 minutes. Remove from the heat and carefully pass through a food mill or press through a sieve to remove all the seeds and skin.

Measure the purée and then return it to the saucepan. Measure an equal amount of sugar and add it to the pan. Stirring constantly, bring to a boil over high heat, and then decrease the heat to medium to achieve a simmer. Cook for 20 to 25 minutes, until it "blows a rose": Dip a spoon into the mixture and blow on the back of the spoon. If it creates the shape of a rose and holds that shape as it cools, it is done. If not, continue to simmer for another 5 minutes and test again. Remove from the heat and stir in the orange zest.

Place a large metal spoon in a heatproof bowl to distribute the heat of the sauce. Very carefully pour or ladle the cranberry mixture into the bowl. Remove the spoon, cover the bowl, and refrigerate overnight before serving.

Carrot Ring

SERVES 4 TO 6

This is a tasty, creative alternative to a regular vegetable side dish. Baked in a ring pan, you can fill the center with fresh herbs or edible flowers for a beautiful presentation.

1/2 cup high-quality vegetable shortening
1/2 cup firmly packed light brown sugar
2 eggs, separated
2 cups finely grated carrot
1 tablespoon water
1 tablespoon freshly squeezed orange juice
1 cup sifted flour
1/2 teaspoon salt
1/2 teaspoon baking soda
1 teaspoon baking powder

Preheat the oven to 350°. Butter and flour a 6-cup ring mold.

In a large bowl, combine the shortening and sugar. With an electric mixer on high speed, beat together until creamy and light. Add the egg yolks, carrot, water, and orange juice and beat until combined. Sift together the flour, salt, baking soda, and baking powder in another bowl. In a third bowl, with clean beaters on high speed, beat the egg whites until soft peaks form. Fold the flour mixture into the carrot mixture until fully incorporated. Fold the combined mixture into the egg whites. Pour into the prepared pan.

Bake for 15 minutes. Increase the oven temperature to 375° and continue to bake for 20 minutes, until a toothpick comes out dry. Remove from the oven and allow to rest in the pan for 10 minutes. Turn out of the pan onto a serving plate, cut into 2-inch-wide slices, and serve immediately.

Toasted Coconut Layer Cake

SERVES 8 TO 10

Served on a pretty footed plate, this cake makes a great—and tasty—centerpiece for a dessert table. The Sisters particularly like the cake because sweetened coconut not only covers the top and sides, but also is folded right into the frosting.

2¼ cups cake flour
1½ teaspoons baking powder
1 teaspoon salt
¼ cup unsalted butter, at room temperature
½ cup high-quality vegetable shortening, at room temperature
1½ cups granulated sugar
3 eggs
¾ cup milk
1 teaspoon pure vanilla extract
½ teaspoon pure almond extract

FROSTING
1 pound sweetened flaked coconut
1½ cups unsalted butter, at room temperature
1½ cups high-quality vegetable shortening, at room temperature
1 tablespoon pure vanilla extract
2 pounds (4 cups) confectioners' sugar

Preheat the oven to 350°. Butter and flour 3 round cake pans, each 9 inches in diameter.

To prepare the cake, sift together the flour, baking powder, and salt into a large bowl. In another bowl, combine the butter, shortening, and granulated sugar. With an electric mixer on high speed, beat together until light and airy. Add the eggs and whip again. With the mixer on low speed, slowly add the milk, vanilla, and almond extract. Fold in the flour mixture. Divide the batter evenly among the 3 prepared pans.

Bake for 20 to 25 minutes, until a toothpick inserted into the center comes out dry. Allow to cool for 10 minutes in the pans on cooling racks and then invert onto the racks to cool completely. Leave the oven set at 350°.

To prepare the frosting, spread half of the coconut on a baking sheet. Toast for 10 to 15 minutes, until golden brown. Remove from the oven and allow to cool.

In a bowl, combine the butter and shortening. With the electric mixer on high speed, beat until smooth. Add the vanilla and then the confectioners' sugar and continue to beat until light and fluffy. Fold in the untoasted coconut, mixing well.

To assemble the cake, place 1 cake layer on an attractive serving plate. Spread one-quarter of the frosting over the top. Top with another layer and repeat with another one-quarter of the frosting. Top with the third layer and use the remaining frosting to frost the top and sides of the cake. Immediately after frosting, press the toasted coconut onto the top and sides of the cake. Any extra frosting can be piped into rosettes on top. Slice and serve immediately.

In addition to cooking for forty-odd Sisters in the main dining room, I also prepare meals for the infirmary, which houses not only the oldest of the Sisters, but also anyone recovering from an illness or an injury. The immediate female relatives of the Sisters, such as mothers, sisters, and cousins, who have no one else to care for them are also invited to come and live in the infirmary.

Usually ten or so patients are in residence at any given time. While the menu is generally the same as for the main dining room, I try to add certain items that might be easier to digest. Health shakes made with calorie- and

✠ *Hannah and Sister Flavia. Whose day is longer?*

nutrition-enhancing ingredients have become popular, as have homemade soups and custards.

My children Matthew and Hannah have become small ambassadors of good will to the infirmary. Several times a week, they visit the "special" Sisters, as Matthew calls them. He delivers the mail to their rooms and greets each of them by name with a bright three-year-old "hello!" Hannah adds her two cents, by giggling and cooing at every hello and goodbye. Her first wave of "bye-bye" was enjoyed by all.

Despite their age or poor health, these Sisters, who hold the history of the order in their collective memories, remain a vital part of the community. They also host the best Halloween and Valentine's Day parties that I have been to in a long time.

DECEMBER

The most magical month of the year is here. The halls are filled with the sounds of the choir practicing for Midnight Mass, and all of the Sisters are trying to get their Christmas shopping done. With luck, we have had the first heavy snowfall and the grounds of the convent look like a winter wonderland. The outside of the buildings are festooned with large wreaths made of fragrant evergreen and bright red ribbons, and huge pots of brilliantly colored poinsettias line the halls.

The church is decorated the week before Christmas. Large, full fir trees are brought in to decorate the altar, and each one is studded with hundreds of tiny white lights. The only other decoration is a large replica of the manger in which Jesus spent his first night. All the figures are in place: Mary, Joseph, and the shepherds with their flocks. The three wise men approach from the east, and there is even an angel to harken the coming of the Christ child. The only figure missing is the tiny baby Jesus. He doesn't appear until his birthday at midnight on Christmas Eve, when the whole community is there to welcome him with songs and prayers.

The kitchen is a swirl of activity in preparation for the holidays. Cookies and cakes seem to flow like rivers, both going out of my oven and coming in from all of the friends and family that care so much about the Sisters. Three of my favorite holiday desserts are included in this chapter, as well as some spectacular entrées and side dishes for your holiday meals.

December 6, the feast of Saint Nicholas, is an important feast day at the convent, almost a junior Christmas. The Sisters decorate the dining room with pretty tablecloths and holiday napkins. They put carols on the stereo, light candles on each table, and enjoy one another's company before the hubbub of the season really gets started. I sometimes serve a mulled cider punch on this day. The Sisters like to sip it while enjoying the special cookies and cakes I have made.

Each Christmas Eve, the Sisters forgo a traditional sit-down dinner and instead have a festive holiday cocktail party. While I prepare a variety of cold meat platters, salads, and various finger foods, any of the Sisters that feel up to the task prepare their own hors d'oeuvres for the party. After they have eaten their fill of the offerings, they repair to the church to participate in the Christmas Eve vigil followed by Midnight Mass. There is nothing as inspiring as sitting in a church full of truly happy and excited people awaiting Christ's birthday. At the stroke of midnight, the bell in the church's steeple sounds the arrival of Christ's feast day and all the voices in the community join together to sing joyful hymns in celebration. It is an experience not soon forgotten.

Continuing in this spirit, I hope that your holidays, both in and out of the kitchen, will also be a ringing success.

The Whole Chicken Soup

SERVES 6 TO 8

Each year, December brings the first round of the flu, and every one of the Sisters catches it in some form. Some of them blame the dry heat, some the dripping noses of their students, but they all suffer the same. This soup has garlic to boost the immune system and ginger to fight nausea. The recipe makes a lot, so you can portion it out and freeze it for whenever the need arises, and believe me it will.

1 (3-pound) chicken
1 bunch fresh parsley
1 lemon, halved
15 black peppercorns
4 cloves garlic, crushed
2-inch piece fresh ginger, peeled and crushed
4 chicken-flavored bouillon cubes
2 yellow onions, quartered
4 carrots, peeled and cut into 6 pieces
4 celery stalks, cut into 6 pieces
2 cups ditalini or other small pasta shape, boiled until al dente and drained
Salt
Freshly ground black pepper
Grated Romano cheese, for serving (optional)

Rinse the chicken under cold running water. Place in a large soup pot and add cold water to cover. Pull the leaves off the parsley stems, reserving both. Chop the leaves and set aside.

To prepare a bouquet garni, fold a 6-inch-square piece of cheesecloth in half and place the parsley stems, lemon halves, peppercorns, garlic, and ginger on it. Bring the corners of the cheesecloth together and tie securely with kitchen string, leaving a long loose end. Add the bouquet garni to the soup pot, tying the loose end to the handle. Make sure it is well submerged. Bring to a boil over high heat. Decrease the heat to medium and simmer, skimming off foam as it forms, for $1^1/_2$ to 2 hours, until the meat falls off the bones. Continue to add water as needed to keep the chicken immersed.

Remove the chicken and bouquet garni from the pot, being careful to capture the juices that drain off both. Place the chicken on a large baking sheet and let stand until cool enough to handle, pouring any accumulated juices back into the pot. Pull the chicken meat from the bones.

Pass the broth through a fine-mesh sieve to remove any solids and return to the pot over medium heat. Add the bouillon cubes, onions, carrots, and celery. Bring to a simmer and cook for 30 minutes, until the vegetables are soft. Add the chicken meat and the pasta and stir in the reserved chopped parsley. Simmer until heated through. Season with salt and pepper.

To serve, ladle the soup into warmed soup bowls. Serve piping hot and pass the cheese at the table.

Baked Honey-Glazed Ham

SERVES 6 TO 8

A honey-glazed ham always seems like perfect fare for Christmas Day dinner. I glaze the ham twice, once before I put it in the oven and again right after I take it out. Then I let it rest for twenty minutes before slicing, so that the juices stay in the ham rather then running all over the cutting board.

1 (3-pound) cured and sugared ham, preferably boneless
2 cups honey
1/2 cup spicy dark mustard
1/4 cup cornstarch
1 teaspoon ground cloves
16 pineapple slices
16 maraschino cherries, stemmed

Preheat the oven to 350°. Line a large roasting pan with aluminum foil for quick cleanup. Place a rack in the pan or make a ring with crumpled foil and place in the pan to serve as a rack. With a sharp knife, score the top of the ham lengthwise and then crosswise, creating small diamonds on the surface.

In a bowl, combine the honey, mustard, cornstarch, and cloves. Drizzle about half of the glaze over the meat and massage into the skin. Using toothpicks, secure a pineapple slice on top of the ham with a cherry in the center. Repeat until the ham is covered with pineapple-cherry rings. Place in the oven and roast, uncovered, for 60 to 90 minutes, until golden brown and the temperature registers 150°. Remove from the oven and let rest for 5 minutes. Brush with the remaining glaze and allow to rest for at least 20 minutes before slicing.

Remove the pineapple and cherries and reserve to garnish each serving. To serve, slice the ham thinly and lay 2 slices on each diner's plate. Arrange the roasted fruit to the side of the ham slices.

Mediterranean Flounder with Tomatoes and Olives

SERVES 6

On Christmas Eve, Catholics refrain from eating meat. Traditionally, several fish courses are served. When my grandmother prepared this Feast of the Twelve Fishes for Christmas Eve, one of the dishes she made was baccalà, or salted cod, prepared with tomatoes and onions and big juicy black olives thrown in at the end. This recipe is made with simple flounder or sole fillets, but is equally delicious.

1/4 cup olive oil
4 cloves garlic, peeled and minced
2 yellow onions, chopped
2 (28-ounce) cans Italian-style diced tomatoes
1 cup fish stock (page 200), or 1 (8-ounce) bottle clam juice
Salt
1/4 teaspoon crushed red pepper flakes, plus extra for garnish
1 (16-ounce) can pitted jumbo black olives
6 (8-ounce) flounder or sole fillets, skin on

Place a saucepan over high heat and add the olive oil. When the oil is hot, add the garlic and onions and sauté for 5 minutes, until aromatic. Add the tomatoes, stock, salt to taste, and pepper flakes. Decrease the heat to medium and simmer for 20 minutes, until slightly thickened. Add the olives and simmer for 20 minutes longer, until the flavors incorporate.

Meanwhile, preheat the oven to 350°. Grease the bottom of a glass or ceramic baking dish with olive oil. Rinse the fish under cold running water and pat dry with paper towels. Run your fingertips along the flesh to make sure all the bones have been removed. Fold the fillets in half crosswise, skin side in, and arrange in the prepared baking dish. When the sauce is ready, pour it over the fillets and cover the dish with aluminum foil. Bake for 20 minutes, until the flesh flakes when pressed gently with a fork.

To serve, place 1 fillet on each diner's plate. Ladle the sauce and olives over the top. For added zing, garnish each serving with a pinch of red pepper flakes.

For the daily meals, whether at noon or at mid afternoon,
it is enough, we believe, to provide all the tables with two kinds
of cooked food because of individual weakness. In this way,
a person who may not be able to eat one kind of food may partake
of another.

—The Rule of Saint Benedict, chapter 39

Candied Sweet Potatoes

SERVES 4 TO 6

The Sisters appreciate the fact that I use fresh sweet potatoes as opposed to canned ones for this recipe. Fresh potatoes make such a big difference in the final taste. This is a good recipe for busy December, as it can be prepared up to the baking stage, covered, and placed in the fridge overnight.

4 large sweet potatoes, unpeeled
1/4 cup unsalted butter
1/4 cup thawed orange juice concentrate
Grated zest of 1 orange
Juice of 1 orange
1 cup firmly packed brown sugar
1 tablespoon ground cinnamon
1 tablespoon granulated sugar

Place the sweet potatoes in a large pot and add cold water to cover. Place over high heat and bring to a boil. Decrease the heat to medium and simmer, uncovered, for 10 to 15 minutes, until fork tender. Drain and allow to cool. Peel the sweet potatoes and cut into 2-inch pieces.

Preheat the oven to 350°. Grease a 9 by 13-inch baking dish with butter. Arrange the potatoes in a single layer in the prepared baking dish. Cut the butter into small pieces and sprinkle evenly around the potatoes. In a small bowl, combine the orange juice concentrate, orange zest, and orange juice. Pour evenly over the potatoes. Crumble the brown sugar evenly over the surface. Mix together the cinnamon and granulated sugar and sprinkle on top.

Place in the oven and bake, uncovered, for 30 to 40 minutes, until the potatoes are very soft and a golden brown crust forms on the outside. Remove from the oven and cover loosely to keep warm. Serve warm.

Sweet-and-Sour Red Cabbage

SERVES 4 TO 6

Nowadays, this dish is rarely made from scratch, with most cooks instead turning to a can. This recipe is low in fat and calories, is very easy to prepare, and smells great while it is cooking.

3 tablespoons vegetable oil
1 yellow onion, chopped
2 green apples, peeled, cored, and diced
1 head red cabbage, cored and thinly sliced
1/2 cup cider vinegar
1/2 cup sugar
1 cinnamon stick
1 tablespoon salt
1/2 teaspoon freshly ground black pepper
1 teaspoon caraway seeds
2 tablespoons flour
1/4 cup water

In a large pot over high heat, warm the oil. Add the onion and apples and sauté for 5 minutes, until soft. Add the cabbage, vinegar, sugar, cinnamon stick, salt, pepper, and caraway seeds and stir well. Cover, decrease the heat to medium, and simmer, stirring frequently, for 30 minutes, until the cabbage is tender.

In a small bowl, stir together the flour and water. Add to the cabbage and stir well. Cover, decrease the heat to low, and simmer slowly for 20 minutes, until the liquid has thickened. Remove and discard the cinnamon stick. Transfer to a decorative serving bowl and serve hot.

Classic Tiramisu

SERVES 6 TO 8

You may need to lie down on the floor while eating this dessert. Otherwise you may faint and suffer bodily injury, once you discover how delicious it is. The creamy texture of the mascarpone cheese is complemented perfectly by the ladyfingers and espresso coffee. The Sisters describe it as heaven on earth.

6 egg yolks
1 1/4 cups sugar
16 ounces mascarpone cheese, or 2 (8-ounce) packages cream cheese,
    at room temperature
1 3/4 cups heavy cream
1/3 cup coffee-flavored liqueur
2 cups brewed espresso, chilled
2 (16-ounce) packages ladyfingers

GARNISH
2 cups heavy cream
1/4 cup sugar
1 teaspoon pure vanilla extract
Unsweetened cocoa powder, for dusting

To prepare the filling, combine the egg yolks and sugar in a bowl. With an electric mixer on high speed, whip until light, fluffy, and pale yellow. Transfer to the top of a double boiler over barely simmering water and cook, stirring constantly, for 8 minutes, until thick and glossy. Remove from the heat and allow to cool completely while whisking constantly. Add the cheese and continue to whisk until well mixed.

In a large bowl, with the electric mixer on high speed, whip the cream until soft peaks form. Fold the cheese mixture into the whipped cream. In a small, shallow bowl, combine the liqueur and espresso.

Dip a ladyfinger quickly into the coffee mixture and place in the bottom of a tall-sided glass bowl such as a trifle dish. Repeat to form a complete layer of soaked ladyfingers in the bottom of the bowl. Top with one-third of the cheese mixture, spreading it evenly. Repeat the layers 2 more times, until all the ingredients have been used. Cover tightly and refrigerate overnight.

To prepare the garnish, combine the cream, sugar, and vanilla in a bowl. With the electric mixer on high speed, whip until stiff peaks form. Decorate the top of the tiramisu with the whipped cream and, using a sieve, dust with the cocoa powder.

To serve, use a long-handled spoon to scoop out individual portions onto dessert plates.

Cranberry-Nut Bread *(see photo insert)*

MAKES 2 LOAVES

I always bake several loaves of this sweet and tangy bread for the Sisters to enjoy on Christmas morning. The combination of cranberries and orange makes a wonderfully satisfying treat. This bread is also a great gift for nearly anyone on your holiday list.

1 (12-ounce) bag fresh cranberries (3 cups)
2 cups sifted flour
$1^1/_2$ teaspoons baking powder
1 teaspoon baking soda
1 teaspoon salt
1 cup sugar
$^1/_4$ cup chilled unsalted butter
1 egg
$^3/_4$ cup freshly squeezed orange juice
1 tablespoon grated orange zest
$1^1/_2$ cups golden raisins
$1^1/_2$ cups chopped walnuts

Preheat the oven to 350°. Butter and flour 2 loaf pans, each measuring 4 by 8 inches.

Rinse the berries and discard any soft or wrinkled ones. Place in a food processor and pulse about 5 times, until chopped. Remove and measure out $1^1/_2$ cups for the recipe.

Sift together the flour, baking powder, baking soda, and salt into a large bowl. Stir in the sugar. With a pastry blender or 2 butter knives, cut the butter into the dry ingredients until the mixture has the consistency of rolled oats. Add the egg, orange juice, and orange zest and mix well with a wooden spoon. Add the cranberries, raisins, and walnuts and mix well. Divide the batter evenly between the 2 prepared pans.

Bake for 45 to 60 minutes, until a toothpick inserted into the center comes out clean. Remove from the oven and let cool completely in the pans on cooling racks, then turn out of the pans. To serve, cut into 1/2-inch-thick slices.

Strengthen me with raisin cakes,

Refresh me with apples,

For I am faint with love.

—Song of Songs 2:5

Pignoli Cookies *(see photo insert)*

MAKES 36 COOKIES

This cookie recipe has become somewhat of a Christmas signature at the convent, since I make them every year. I have literally made hundreds and hundreds of these cookies, which have been used as gifts for family and friends.

1$1/2$ cups sliced blanched almonds
2 cups granulated sugar
4 tablespoons confectioners' sugar
1 cup flour, or as needed
$1/4$ teaspoon salt
4 egg whites
2$1/2$ cups pine nuts

Line 2 baking sheets with parchment paper.

Place the almonds in a food processor and pulse until finely ground. Transfer to a large bowl and add the granulated sugar, confectioners' sugar, 1 cup flour, and salt. Mix well with a wooden spoon. Add the egg whites and stir until smooth. Add additional flour if the dough seems very sticky.

Spread the pine nuts on a large plate. Drop the dough by tablespoonfuls into the nuts and roll to cover evenly. Place on the prepared baking sheets, spacing the cookies about 3 inches apart. Cover and refrigerate for 1 hour.

Preheat the oven to 350°. Bake the cookies for 18 minutes, until golden. Remove from the oven and let cool completely on the baking sheets on cooling racks. Store in an airtight container for up to 1 week.

The convent is filled with Sisters of all ages and nationalities. Their paths to the convent are equally diverse. The older Sisters are typically immigrant or first-generation Irish or German. Some came to the order as adults, sent from orders in their home countries. Others were taught by the Sisters after coming to this country as children, and ended up joining the order.

Most Sisters that entered in the fifties, sixties, and seventies had a prior relationship with the Benedictine Sisters. Many were students in one of the schools and some were even raised in an orphanage that the Sisters ran. In the past ten years, the new Sisters reflect the diversity of the nearby communities.

For example, Sister Lauren is Vietnamese, and has become an integral part of the convent with her youth and vitality. Sister Lucy is of Cuban decent and is bilingual, enabling her to reach out to the large population of Hispanics in the area. She also teaches the three-year-olds at the preschool. Sister Mariette Therese is the newest arrival on campus, and hopes to be the first of many new Benedictine Sisters of the future.

✠ *Sisters Catherine Marie, Ursula, Rosemary, Patrick, Lauren, Alice, Mariette, Marcia, and Flavia in the gathering space.*

MARIA'S PANTRY

Chicken Stock

MAKES 2 QUARTS

A good stock is the cornerstone for many recipes. Whether used in soups or sauces, for poaching or deglazing, the subtle flavor of your stock will give the recipe a depth of taste and aroma. This and the following two recipes can be multiplied as needed and frozen in small amounts to be used at your convenience. I often fill and freeze an ice-cube tray so I can toss cubes right in as I deglaze a pan or thicken a sauce. It is very important to remember cleanliness when preparing and storing stock. The sieve and container that the finished stock goes into must be very clean or they can transfer bacteria that cause spoilage overnight. Remember to thoroughly wash your hands and any storage containers for the same reason.

5 pounds chicken parts, such as backs, necks, and wings
4 quarts water
10 black peppercorns
2 bay leaves
1/2 bunch parsley
2 carrots, peeled and chopped
3 celery stalks, chopped
2 yellow onions, chopped

Rinse the chicken pieces under cold running water and place in a large pot. Add the water and place over high heat. Bring to a rolling boil and skim off any foam that forms on the surface. Add the peppercorns, bay leaves, parsley, carrots, celery, and onions. Return to a boil and skim the surface again, if necessary. Decrease the heat to low and simmer for at least 3 hours, until the flavors are well developed. Add more water if the stock appears to reduce too quickly.

Remove the stock from the heat and pass through a fine-mesh sieve, discarding the solids. Refrigerate the stock overnight and skim off any congealed fat. Divide into small containers and freeze, or place in the refrigerator for up to 3 days.

Beef Stock

MAKES 2 QUARTS

6 pounds lean shin and marrow bones
3 tablespoons tomato paste
2 cups plus 4 quarts water
10 black peppercorns
2 bay leaves
3 sprigs thyme
1/2 bunch parsley
2 carrots, peeled and chopped
3 celery stalks, chopped
2 tomatoes, chopped
2 yellow onions, chopped

Preheat the oven to 350°. Rinse the bones under cold running water and place in a large roasting pan. Roast for about 45 minutes, until browned. Spread the tomato paste over the bones and toss to coat evenly. Place in the oven and roast for another 15 minutes, until the paste is browned. Remove from the oven and immediately deglaze the pan with the 2 cups water, scraping up any brown bits with a wooden spatula.

Transfer the contents of the roasting pan to a large pot and add the 4 quarts water. Over high heat, bring to a rolling boil and skim off any foam that forms on the surface. Add the peppercorns, bay leaves, thyme, parsley, carrots, celery, tomatoes, and onions. Return to a boil and skim the surface again, if necessary. Decrease the heat to low and simmer for at least 3 hours, until the flavors are well developed. Add more water if the stock appears to reduce too quickly.

Remove the stock from the heat and pass through a fine-mesh sieve, discarding the solids. Refrigerate the stock overnight and skim off any congealed fat. Divide into small containers and freeze, or place in the refrigerator for up to 5 days.

Fish Stock

MAKES 1 QUART

3 pounds white fish, such as flounder or sole
3 tablespoons plus 1/2 cup freshly squeezed lemon juice
2 quarts water
1 bay leaf
5 black peppercorns
1 carrot, peeled and chopped
1 celery stalk, chopped
1 yellow onion, stuck with 2 whole cloves
1 teaspoon salt
1/3 bunch parsley

Rinse the fish under cold running water. Place on a plate and sprinkle with the 3 tablespoons lemon juice. Cover and place in the refrigerator.

In a large pot over high heat, combine the 1/2 cup lemon juice, water, bay leaf, peppercorns, carrot, celery, onion, salt, and parsley. Bring to a rolling boil, then decrease the heat to low. Simmer for 30 minutes, then increase the heat to high and return to a boil. Drop the cold fish into the boiling stock and decrease the heat to medium-low. Simmer for 30 minutes, until the flavors are well developed.

Remove the stock from the heat and pass through a fine-mesh sieve, discarding the solids. Refrigerate the stock overnight. Divide into small containers and freeze, or place in the refrigerator for up to 3 days.

Roasted Bell Peppers

MAKES 2 CUPS

Roasted bell peppers are frequently purchased, but can easily be made at home. Homemade, they have much better flavor than store-bought ones.

4 large bell peppers, any color
2 tablespoons olive oil

Preheat the broiler. Line a broiler pan with aluminum foil. Rinse the peppers under cold running water and pat dry with paper towels. Rub the peppers thoroughly with the olive oil.

Place the peppers on the prepared pan and place under the broiler. Watch carefully and rotate as the skin on the exposed side starts to blister and blacken. When all sides are charred, remove the peppers from the broiler and transfer to a bowl. Place the bowl in a large paper bag and roll down the top to seal tightly. Allow the peppers to cool in the bag for 20 minutes, until cool enough to handle. Remove from the bag and peel off the skin. Cut in half and remove the stem and seeds. Slice into 1/2-inch strips. Serve as is or refrigerate until needed.

Pie Crust

MAKES 2 SINGLE-CRUST PIES, OR 1 DOUBLE-CRUST PIE

When preparing pie crust, always remember cold, cold, cold. The colder the ingredients are kept, the flakier the end product. While I do freely admit to using a frozen prepared pie crust when pressed for time, I can go the from-scratch route by doubling and freezing this dough for future use.

2 cups flour
1 teaspoon salt
2 tablespoons chilled unsalted butter
2/3 cup chilled high-quality vegetable shortening
5 to 6 tablespoons ice water

In a bowl, stir together the flour and salt with a fork. Using a pastry blender or 2 butter knives, cut the butter and shortening into the dry ingredients until the mixture has the consistency of rolled oats. Add the ice water and mix with the fork and then your hands to form the dough into a ball. The dough should just stay together. If it is too dry, add another tablespoon of water. Divide the dough in half. Wrap each half in plastic wrap and press into a 1-inch-thick disk. Place in the refrigerator for 30 minutes.

Unwrap 1 portion of the dough and place on a lightly floured work surface. With a lightly floured rolling pin, roll out into a circle 1/4-inch-thick and roughly 2 inches larger then the pie pan. Transfer the dough to the pie pan and gently press into the bottom and sides. Trim off any excess and pinch or flute the edges. Fill as desired. The other portion of the dough can be prepared the same way, or rolled out to be used as a top crust. (The crust can also be baked blind. Prick the bottom several times with a fork, line with aluminum foil, fill with pie weights or dried beans, and bake at 350° for about 12 minutes, until golden brown.)

Index